plays 2 50

Wild Honey

a comedy by
Michael Frayn
from the play without a name by
Anton Chekhov

3/19

SAMUEL FRENCH, INC.
45 WEST 25TH STREET NEW YORK 10010
7623 SUNSET BOULEVARD HOLLYWOOD 90046
LONDON *TORONTO*

Wild Honey was first presented at the National Theatre, in the Lyttleton, on 19 July 1984, with the following cast:

DR. TRILETZKY, the local doctor. . . . . . Karl Johnson
YAKOV, a servant in the Voynitzev household
. . . . .Peter Dineen
ANNA PETROVNA, the late General Voynitzev's widow
. . . . Charlotte Cornwell
PORFIRY SEMYONOVICH GLAGOLYEV, a local
    landowner . . . . .Basil Henson
SERGEY, Anna Petrovna's stepson . . . . Nicholas Jones
COLONEL TRILETZKY, a retired artillery officer and
    father of Dr. Triletsky and Sasha. . Brewster Mason
SOFYA, Sergey's wife . . . . Elizabeth Garvie
VASILY, another servant . . . . Peter Gordon
MARKO, process server to the local Justice of the
Peace. . . . . Anthony Douse
MARYA YEFIMOVNA GREKOVA, a chemistry student
. . . . Abigail McKern
PLATONOV, the local schoolmaster . . . . Ian McKellen
SASHA, his wife . . . . Heather Tobias
GERASIM KUZMICH PETRIN, a wealthy merchant
. . . . .Gertan Klauber
OSIP, a horsethief. . . . . Roger Lloyd Pack
PEASANTS . . . . Lewis George
                                                Mathew Green

Directed by Christopher Morahan
Settings by John Gunter
Costumes by Deirdre Clancy
Music by Dominic Muldowney
Lighting by Robert Bryan

The action takes place on the Voynitzev family estate, in one of the southern provinces of Russia.

In association with
NT The National Theatre of Great Britain

Duncan C. Weldon   Jerome Minskoff

Robert Fryer   Karl Allison   Douglas Urbanski

Jujamcyn Theaters/Richard G. Wolff

Albert and Anita Waxman

present

IAN McKELLEN

in

WILD HONEY

a comedy by
MICHAEL FRAYN
from the play without a name by
ANTON CHEKHOV

Starring

KATHRYN WALKER

Kate Burton   Kim Cattrall   Franklin Cover

Featuring
Sullivan Brown   J. Smith-Cameron   William Duff-Griffin

George Hall   Frank Maraden   Stephen Mendillo   Jonathan Moore

Vivienne Avramoff   William Cain   Kitty Crooks   Ron Johnston   Timothy Landfield

Scenery by	Costumes by	Lighting by
John Gunter	Deirdre Clancy	Martin Aronstein

Incidental Music by	Casting by	Production Stage Manager
Dominic Muldowney	Howard Feuer	Bob Borod

Entire Production Conceived and Directed by
CHRISTOPHER MORAHAN

Originally presented in the United States by
Center Theatre Group/Ahmanson Theatre, Los Angeles.

The producers wish to express their appreciation
to Theatre Development Fund for its support of this production.

The Producers and Theatre Management are Members
of The League of American Theatres and Producers, Inc.

CAST

(in order of appearance)

Dr. Triletzky, the local doctor .... SULLIVAN BROWN
Yakov, a servant in the Voynitzev household .... TIMOTHY LANDFIELD
Maids .... VIVIENNE AVRAMOFF, KITTY CROOKS
Anna Petrovna, the late General Voynitzev's widow .... KATHRYN WALKER
Porfiry Semyonovich Glagolyev, a local landowner .... JONATHAN MOORE
Sergey, Anna Petrovna's stepson .... FRANK MARADEN
Colonel Triletzky, a retired artillery officer and father
   of Dr. Triletzky and Sasha .... FRANKLIN COVER
Sofya, Sergey's wife .... KIM CATTRALL
Vasily, another servant .... RON JOHNSTON
Marko, process server to the local Justice of the Peace .... GEORGE HALL
Marya Yerfimovna Grekova, a chemistry student .... J. SMITH-CAMERON
Platonov, the local schoolmaster .... IAN McKELLEN
Sasha, his wife .... KATE BURTON
Gerasim Kuzmich Petrin, a wealthy mechant .... WILLIAM DUFF-GRIFFIN
Osip, a horsethief .... STEPHEN MENDILLO
Peasant .... WILLIAM CAIN

The action takes place on the Voynitzev family estate
in one of the southern provinces of Russia.

Standbys and understudies never substitute for listed players unless a specific
announcement is made at the time of the performance.

Standby for Platonov—Guy Paul.

Understudy for Anna Petrovna and Sofya—Vivienne Avramoff; for Sasha and Grekova—
Kitty Crooks; for Colonel Triletzky, Glagolyev, Marko, Vasily and Yakov—William Cain;
for Dr. Triletzky and Osip—Timothy Landfield; for Petrin—Ron Johnston; for Sergey—
Guy Paul.

Wild Honey

ACT ONE

SCENE ONE

*The verandah of the Voynitzevs' country house. It looks
   out on to a sunlit garden, with the tall trees of the
   forest beyond, bisected by a grassy walk.*

*The whoosh of a rocket taking off. The lights come up to
   reveal YAKOV in the garden with a large box of
   assorted fireworks in his arms. Beside him stands
   DR. TRILETZKY, a match in his hand. They are
   gazing up into the sky—DR. TRILETZKY with
   delight, YAKOV with apprehension. There is a smell
   of sulphur in the air. The rocket bursts, off.*

DR. TRILETZKY. Look at it! It's like someone bursting
out laughing! (*The stick falls into the garden.*) Let's set
two off together! (*YAKOV backs away on to the verandah
in alarm, as DR. TRILETZKY begins to light the touch-
papers of the other rockets sticking up from the box.*) Let's
set four off! Let's send the whole lot up!

(*Enter ANNA PETROVNA in alarm.*)

ANNA PETROVNA. Doctor! (*Yakov turns to face
ANNA PETROVNA, still holding the box of fireworks.*)
DR. TRILETZKY. Fireworks!
ANNA PETROVNA. (*to YAKOV*) Outside!
YAKOV. Outside . . . (*He puts the fireworks down
and flees.*)

7

ANNA PETROVNA. Yakov! Come back! Take the fireworks! (*YAKOV picks them up uncertainly.*) Now outside! Quick! Run! (*Exit YAKOV hurriedly with the box. To DR. TRILETZKY:*) For heaven's sake. The whole house will be in flames! (*The sound of a series of rockets departing, off.*)

ANNA PETROVNA. Doctor, really! They're for later! When it gets dark!

DR. TRILETZKY. Anna Petrovna! (*He takes her hand.*) It's all your fault! (*He kisses her hand.*)

ANNA PETROVNA. *My* fault? (*Enter YAKOV, with the blackened box of fireworks, and a blackened face. To YAKOV:*) Take them away! Put them with the others behind the old summerhouse! I told you before. (*Exit YAKOV through the garden.*) *My* fault?

DR. TRILETZKY. Of course! You're back! So we're all quite light-headed. You don't know what it's been like here in the country without you. I can't imagine how we've all survived the winter. Was it wonderful in town? Did you go to the theatre? Did you have dinner in restaurants? Did you miss us all? Are you pleased to be back? Or are you bored already? If you think this place is dull when you're here you should be here when you're *not* here. We all live under dust-covers, like the furniture. But now you're back, and the covers are off, and it's the first perfect day of summer, and when are we going to eat?

ANNA PETROVNA. Not for ages yet. Cook's got drunk to celebrate our arrival . . . Are you feeling my pulse, doctor? Or are you taking a little bite to keep you going until lunchtime?

DR. TRILETZKY. I was just thinking. You arrived last night?

ANNA PETROVNA. On the evening train.

DR. TRILETZKY. Where did you get the fireworks, then?

ANNA PETROVNA. Your father sent them. He came over first thing this morning.

DR. TRILETZKY. He's shameless! He could have waited until lunch, like the rest of us. He is coming to lunch?

ANNA PETROVNA. Of course. We must have the colonel.

DR. TRILETZKY. And Porfiry Semyonovich is here already. I meet him in the garden with your stepson.

ANNA PETROVNA. Poor Sergey! But I endured him for an hour or more first.

DR. TRILETZKY. So you'll have us all at your feet again. Just like last summer.

(*GLAGOLYEV appears in the garden, making frequent halts to lean on his stick and pontificate to VOYNIT-ZEV, who listens with perfect deference.*)

ANNA PETROVNA. Here comes Porfiry Semyonovich now.

DR. TRILETZKY. He was telling Sergey about the decline in modern manners when I met them.

ANNA PETROVNA. What a cruel stepmother I am!

GLAGOLYEV. (*to VOYNITZEV*) No, we had real respect for them, you see.

VOYNITZEV. Like the knights of old.

GLAGOLYEV. We looked up to them.

VOYNITZEV. You put them on a pedestal.

GLAGOLYEV. We put them on a pedestal.

DR. TRILETZKY. I think they've got on the subject of women.

GLAGOLYEV. We loved women, certainly. But we

loved them in the way that the knights of old loved them.

VOYNITZEV. You had respect for them.

GLAGOLYEV. We had respect for them.

DR. TRILETZKY. Your stepson has become the most agreeable of men.

ANNA PETROVNA. Poor Sergey!

DR. TRILETZKY. He goes away an artist and poet. He comes back with his beard shaved off—and underneath he's not an artist and poet at all! He's a very agreeable young man like everybody else.

ANNA PETROVNA. He doesn't need an artistic nature now. He has a wife instead.

GLAGOLYEV. (*to VOYNITZEV*) So you see, we poor old setting stars have the advantage of you young rising stars!

VOYNITZEV. You knew the world when the world was young.

DR. TRILETZKY. All your old admirers! However will you bear it? Where's Platonov? You'll never put up with us all without Platonov here to amuse you.

ANNA PETRONOV. I've sent across for him twice already. (*GLAGOLYEV and VOYNITZEV approach the verandah.*)

GLAGOLYEV. (*to VOYNITZEV*) No, we believed in women, we worshipped the ground they walked on, because we saw in woman the better part of man . . .

DR. TRILETZKY. I'll tell Vasily to run over there again. (*Exit DR. TRILETZKY. GLAGOLYEV and VOYNITZEV come in from the garden.*)

GLAGOLYEV. Anna Petrovna! We were just talking about the fair sex, as chance would have it.

ANNA PETROVNA. You have always given the subject a great deal of time and attention.

GLAGOLYEV. I was saying to your stepson that woman

is the better part of man. Or so we believed in my day. So your late husband believed, I know that, God rest his soul. (*to VOYNITZEV*) Oh yes, your father was like me, God give him peace—one of the old school, the General . . . So hot! I must sit down, I'm quite done up . . . (*COLONEL TRILETZKY appears in the garden, leaning on a stick like GLAGOLYEV.*)

VOYNITZEV. And here's the colonel.

GLAGOLYEV. The colonel, was it, who sent those fireworks? Dangerous things, fireworks. I'm no great lover of fireworks. (*COLONEL TRILETZKY comes in from the garden.*)

COLONEL TRILETZKY. (*to ANNA PETROVNA*) Your Majesty!

ANNA PETROVNA. Colonel!

COLONEL TRILETZKY. A twenty-one gun salute to the queen of the district! (*He raises the stick into his shoulder.*) Bang bang bang! Bang bang . . . !

VOYNITZEV. Colonel! Still ready with a salvo?

COLONEL TRILETZKY. Sergey Pavlovich!

VOYNITZEV. You're well, are you?

COLONEL TRILETZKY. I'm always well. The good Lord endures me with remarkable patience. Porfiry Semyonovich!

GLAGOLYEV. (*disgusted*) Fireworks!

COLONEL TRILETZKY. (*to ANNA PETROVNA*) Arrived, have they?

ANNA PETROVNA. So kind of you. Something for us all to look forward to.

COLONEL TRILETZKY. Only supporting fire I can provide these days.

GLAGOLYEV. He'll blow you all up if you're not careful.

COLONEL TRILETZKY. A twenty-one rocket salute!

(*He raises the stick to his shoulder.*)

(*Enter DR. TRILETZKY.*)

Dr. Triletzky. Don't shoot! It's your long-lost son!

Colonel Triletzky. Kolya!

Dr. Triletzky. And in the nick of time, by the look of it.

Colonel Triletzky. (*lowers his stick, and embraces DR. TRILETZKY with emotion*) My dear boy!

Dr. Triletzky. Father!

Colonel Triletzky. Haven't seen you for . . . what . . . ?

Dr. Triletzky. It must be nearly two weeks now, Father.

Colonel Triletzky. Have to come to Anna Petrovna's to see my own son! Keep meaning to call on you. Never manage it. Too busy!

Dr. Triletzky. (*to ANNA PETROVNA*) Summer again, and your little court is assembling for the season.

Anna Petrovna. It's not me you've all come to see this time. It's my new daughter-in-law.

Dr. Triletzky. (*to VOYNITZEV*) Yes! Where is she?

Colonel Triletzky. Of course! He's got married! There's my memory for you!

Anna Petrovna. (*to VOYNITZEV*) Everyone's longing to meet her.

Colonel Triletzky. But what a funny fellow! Gets married, and never says a word about it! Talks about nothing but guns! Well, life and happiness to you, Sergey Pavlovich! Life and happiness! Is she beautiful?

Anna Petrovna. Enchanting!

Colonel Triletzky. Two queens on the board against us! We're done for!

DR. TRILETZKY. Fetch her out, then! It's not fair to keep us all in suspense.

ANNA PETROVNA. Especially Porfiry Semyonovich. He's such a great lover of women.

GLAGOLYEV. I certainly prefer them to sporting guns and fireworks.

VOYNITZEV. I think she's walking under the trees. I'll see if I can find her. (*VOYNITZEV goes out into the garden.*)

COLONEL TRILETZKY. (*takes ANNA PETROVNA's hand*) This is the girl for me, though!

ANNA PETROVNA. (*to DR. TRILETZKY*) Your father's going to take me quail-shooting.

GLAGOLYEV. If you are interested in birds, I could show you several quite rare species on my estate.

DR. TRILETZKY. (*to ANNA PETROVNA*) They're fighting over you!

ANNA PETROVNA. (*a hand on both their arms*) We'll all come and see your birds. We'll bring the colonel's new twelve-bore.

COLONEL TRILETZKY. God strike me down, but this is the girl for me! The emancipation of women in person, this one! Get a sniff of her shoulder! Powder! A warrior-chief, if ever I saw one! Put a pair of epaulettes on her and she'd outgeneral the lot of us!

GLAGOLYEV. Have you been drinking already, colonel?

COLONEL TRILETZKY. Of course I have! Started at eight o'clock this morning! Came over here—found everyone asleep apart from the empress herself. Couldn't have been more delighted to see me, so we split a bottle of Madeira.

ANNA PETROVNA. You didn't have to tell everyone!

GLAGOLYEV. When you come to visit me we shall sample a glass of my housekeeper's whortleberry liqueur.

(*Enter VOYNITZEV and SOFYA through the garden.*)

DR. TRILETZKY. And here she is! (*VOYNITZEV stops to present SOFYA with a flower. They laugh together.*)

DR. TRILETZKY. Oh, but she's an absolute bullseye!

ANNA PETROVNA. I told you!

GLAGOLYEV. Charming couple.

DR. TRILETZKY. The ideal stepson.

ANNA PETROVNA. And the ideal wife for him. (*VOYNITZEV and SOFYA come in from the garden.*)

SOFYA. Oh, Anna Petrovna, I've never seen such a beautiful garden! I'm quite dizzy with sunlight and the scent of flowers! And I've been walking in the forest. It's so cool under the trees, and there's a kind of faint sound in the air all the time, as if the forest were sighing to itself with pure happiness. I can't imagine living in such a place.

ANNA PETROVNA. Well, now you do, my dear.

SOFYA. Do I really?

VOYNITZEV. It's all yours.

SOFYA. It's like a dream! I'm afraid I shall reach out to touch it and everything will vanish.

COLONEL TRILETZKY. Aren't you going to introduce us?

ANNA PETROVNA. Oh, yes. Now. Sofya, these are your new neighbours. The colonel . . .

COLONEL TRILETZKY. Triletzky, Ivan Ivanovich.

ANNA PETROVNA. Who will take you duck-shooting at dawn . . .

COLONEL TRILETZKY. Snipe! The mighty swamp on Porfiry Semyonovich's estate must be full of them! A great polar expedition! We'll all go!

ANNA PETROVNA. Sofya Yegorovna. And this is the colonel's son . . .

DR. TRILETZKY. Nikolai Ivanovich.

ANNA PETROVNA. He's the local doctor, who will nurse you back to health again afterwards. And this is Porfiry Semyonovich, the owner of the mighty swamp. He is . . . what are you, Porfiry Semyonovich? He is a great lover of women.

SOFYA. Really?

GLAGOLYEV. I make the claim in all humility.

SOFYA. And Platonov. Isn't he here?

VOYNITZEV. Yes—Sofya knows Platonov!

SOFYA. Only slightly.

VOYNITZEV. But isn't that extraordinary?

SOFYA. I don't suppose he'll know me.

DR. TRILETZKY. Of course he will! Platonov knows everything.

COLONEL TRILETZKY. He certain knows all the pretty women!

GLAGOLYEV. Really, colonel! We're talking about a serious scholar!

COLONEL TRILETZKY. Our local Socrates!

ANNA PETROVNA. (*to DR. TRILETZKY*) Where is he?

DR. TRILETZKY. I sent Vasily running.

SOFYA. He was a student when I met him. I was only a schoolgirl. He won't remember me.

VOYNITZEV. We'll see! We won't introduce you. We'll find out what kind of scholar he really is!

SOFYA. Oh, but it's so lovely here!

(*Enter VASILY.*)

DR. TRILETZKY. The perfect picture of country life! We're only missing one thing . . .

ANNA PETROVNA. Yes, is he coming, Vasily?

VASILY. Directly, he says, Anna Petrovna, but Anna Petrovna, it's Marko.

ANNA PETROVNA. Marko?

VASILY. From the magistrate, Anna Petrovna.

ANNA PETROVNA. Marko the process-server?

DR. TRILETZKY. What, with a summons?

VASILY. Big envelope, it is.

VOYNITZEV. (*to ANNA PETROVNA*) He's done it! He's taken us to court!

SOFYA. Who? Platonov?

ANNA PETROVNA. No. No one.

DR. TRILETZKY. Someone who lent money to the old general.

VOYNITZEV. He's suing us for it! We've lost the estate!

ANNA PETROVNA. Don't be ridiculous. It's all some silly mistake. (*to VASILY*) Send the man in.

VASILY. This way . . .

(*Enter MARKO, an old man with a neat, soldierly bearing. He has an envelope in his hands, and more envelopes in a satchel round his neck.*)

DR. TRILETZKY. (*to SOFYA*) The old general was sick.

MARKO. Anna Petrovna Voynitzeva?

COLONEL TRILETZKY. (*to SOFYA*) He signed anything they put in front of him.

ANNA PETROVNA. Give to me, then. (*MARKO hands her the envelope.*) I'll open it later.

VOYNITZEV. (*to MARKO*) Yes, you come bursting in

here, badgering my stepmother in front of her guests . . .

MARKO. Sergey Pavlovich Voynitzev?

VOYNITZEV. Yes? (*MARKO hands him another envelope. He gazes at it in astonishment.*)

DR. TRILETZKY. Sergey! What have you been up to?

MARKO. Dr. Nikolai Ivanovich Triletzky?

DR. TRILETZKY. Me? (*MARKO hands him an envelope. He gazes at it in astonishment in his turn.*)

ANNA PETROVNA. You, too?

GLAGOLYEV. My dear Anna Petrovna, if you will allow me to be of assistance . . .

MARKO. Porfiry Semyonovich Glagolyev?

GLAGOLYEV. I beg your pardon?

ANNA PETROVNA. Not you! (*MARKO hands him an envelope. He gazes at it, flabbergasted. They all look at each other's envelopes.*) What, have we all got one, then?

COLONEL TRILETZKY. Not me! Wouldn't do it to an old soldier! Old soldier yourself, aren't you?

MARKO. Artillery, sir.

COLONEL TRILETZKY. Thought so! Corporal Marko, wasn't it?

MARKO. That's it, sir. And you're Colonel Triletzky?

COLONEL TRILETZKY. That's right!

MARKO. Colonel Ivan Ivanovich Triletzky?

COLONEL TRILETZKY. Exactly! (*MARKO hands him an envelope.*) Not a man left standing!

ANNA PETROVNA. Look at Sofya staring.

SOFYA. No, no!

ANNA PETROVNA. I suppose we'd better open them.

(They open them. GREKOVA appears in the garden. She stops, awkward and flustered, to dab a handkerchief

to her face. DR. TRILETZKY is the only one to notice her.)

DR. TRILETZKY. (*goes to meet her*) Marya Yefimovna!

ANNA PETROVNA. (*reads*) 'His Imperial Majesty's Justice of the Peace . . . '

VOYNITZEV. (*reads*) ' . . . will be at home on Sunday June the fifteenth . . . '

GLAGOLYEV. (*reads*) ' . . . on the occasion of his son's christening . . . '

ANNA PETROVNA. It's not a summons!

MARKO. No, ma'am.

COLONEL TRILETZKY. It's an invitation!

MARKO. Yes sir.

DR. TRILETZKY. (*brings GREKOVA into the room*) It's Marya Yefimovna . . . (*The others look up from their letters, and burst out laughing with relief. GREKOVA takes one horrified look at them, and flees back into the garden*).

ANNA PETROVNA. Oh dear. What an unfortunate moment to choose!

COLONEL TRILETZKY. Poor girl! Comes seven miles on a hot afternoon, and what happens? Gets her head blown off! Same thing every time she comes here. Walks in — head blown off.

VOYNITZEV. It's usually Platonov who does it.

ANNA PETROVNA. He's not even here, and already she's hiding under the trees again. It's just like last year.

COLONEL TRILETZKY. Never get her back now.

DR. TRILETZKY. (*looking at his letter*) A christening . . . I suppose I should try . . .

SOFYA. I'll go. I know what it's like, coming into a room full of people. (*SOFYA goes out into the garden, followed by VOYNITZEV.*)

GLAGOLYEV. Charming young woman!

ANNA PETROVNA. Go and help her, Porfiry Semyonovich.

COLONEL TRILETZKY. We'll all go and help her! (*To MARKO.*) And we'll all come to the christening on Sunday! The siege of Sevastopol?

MARKO. And Balaclava, sir.

COLONEL TRILETZKY. See it in your eyes. (*He gives him a coin.*)

MARKO. Thank you, sir. (*GLAGOLYEV and COLONEL TRILETZKY go into the garden.*)

DR. TRILETZKY. I'd better go and talk to her.

ANNA PETROVNA. I think you'd better stay and talk to me. (*to VASILY*) Take him out to the kitchen and give him something to drink. Fancy telling us he was bringing a summons! (*Exeunt VASILY and MARKO.*) So it wasn't me you came to see and it wasn't Sofya! It was your Marya Yefimovna.

DR. TRILETZKY. Anna Petrovna, I was sure she wouldn't come! I thought she'd refused to set foot in the same house as Platonov again, after all that business last summer.

ANNA PETROVNA. I like her! I love her sharp little nose. Is she still studying chemistry?

DR. TRILETZKY. She reads books, too. (*They watch her from the verandah. COLONEL TRILETZKY and GLAGOLYEV approach her, but are taken discreetly aside by VOYNITZEV, leaving SOFYA to stroll with her under the trees.*)

ANNA PETROVNA. Are you serious about her?

DR. TRILETZKY. Platonov thinks she's a fool. That's what the trouble was last summer. He's got it into that unkempt head of his that he has some kind of mission in life to rebuke fools.

ANNA PETROVNA. I know what a fool *you* are. Plenty

of brains in that head of yours, but they're not always much in evidence. *Are* you serious?

DR. TRILETZKY. I call on her nearly every day. I make conversation, I endure the boredom, I put her poor mother to some expense in coffee, and there we are. I talk about what interests me; she talks about what interests her. Then she takes hold of me by the lapels, and brushes the dust off my collar. I always seem to be covered in dust. But quite what draws me back each time, whether it's love or whether it's boredom, I don't really know. (*pause*) All I know is that I miss her quite painfully after lunch sometimes.

ANNA PETROVNA. So it's love, then. And here he is.

(*PLATONOV and SASHA appear in the garden.*)

VOYNITZEV. Platonov!

COLONEL TRILETZKY. Mishenka! My dear fellow!

PLATONOV. Sergey Pavlovich! (*Joyful kisses and handclasps are exchanged.*)

VOYNITZEV. You've put on weight!

PLATONOV. You've taken off your beard.

VOYNITZEV. (*to SASHA*) Alexandra Ivanovna!

PLATONOV. (*shakes hands with GLAGOLYEV*) Porfiry Semyonovich.

GLAGOLYEV. We've been talking about you, Platonov.

COLONEL TRILETZKY. Late on parade again!

PLATONOV. Colonel!

COLONEL TRILETZKY. Keeping Her Majesty waiting!

ANNA PETROVNA. (*to DR. TRILETZKY*) Now we shall be all right.

(*VOYNITZEV, COLONEL TRILETZKY and GLA-*

GOLYEV escort PLATONOV and SASHA on to the verandah in triumph.)

PLATONOV. At last — we're away from home! Anna Petrovna . . . !

VOYNITZEV. Here he is!

COLONEL TRILETZKY. This is the man!

PLATONOV. Say hello to everyone, Sasha . . . Anna Petrovna! (*He takes both her hands and kisses them.*)

ANNA PETROVNA. Cruel man! How could you make us wait so long? You must have known how impatient I should be. Alexandra Ivanovna! My dear! (*She kisses SASHA.*)

PLATONOV. Out of our house at last! Glory be to God! We haven't seen high ceilings for six whole months! We haven't seen people! We've been hibernating in our lair like two old bears, and we've only crawled forth into the world today!

VOYNITZEV. And Alexandra Ivanovna! Are you well?

PLATONOV. She's fine, she's find. And her ladyship's household physician is in attendance, I see. (*He embraces DR. TRILETZKY.*) Radiant with health, by the look of it. Drenched in perfume, by the smell of it. And that haircut must have cost you a ruble or two.

DR. TRILETZKY. You should be pleased to have a well turned-out brother-in-law.

ANNA PETROVNA. But how are you both? Sit down! Tell us everything! We'll all sit down.

PLATONOV. (*to VOYNITZEV, laughing*) Is this really you? Heavens above! Where's the beard and the long hair?

SASHA. Sergey Pavlovich, I must just say one thing . . .

PLATONOV. Sasha, my love, will you never stop talking?

SASHA. (*to VOYNITZEV*) Congratulations.

PLATONOV. Oh, yes! Of course!

SASHA. May I wish you every possible happiness?

PLATONOV. You've got yourself married! My warmest congratulations, too! (*He bows.*) Love and harmony all your days! Who is the lady?

VOYNITZEV. You'll see.

PLATONOV. I must confess I never expected it of you. Rather an about-face for a man of your views.

VOYNITZEV. Well, you know me. Didn't think twice! Fell in love — married her!

PLATONOV. We've had the falling in love part every winter. It's the getting married that's such a novel departure. Have you found a job?

VOYNITZEV. I've been offered a job in a high school of sorts, and I don't know what to do. It's not what I should have chosen.

PLATONOV. You'll take it, though?

VOYNITZEV. I really don't know. Probably not.

PLATONOV. So you'll be letting more time slip by. Three years now, isn't it, since you left university? You need someone to give you a bit of a kick. I must have a word with your wife. Three good years wasted! Isn't that right?

DR. TRILETZKY. He hasn't been in the house five minutes, and already he's flying us all!

GLAGOLYEV. Well, it's rare enough these days — someone with clear moral standards.

COLONEL TRILETZKY. My own son-in-law — the village Savonarola!

ANNA PETROVNA. (*to PLATONOV*) Yes, go on! How have we got through the winter without your moral refreshment?

PLATONOV. It's too hot today to be serious. And it's far too pleasant sitting here again to be indignant at the evils of the world . . . I can see Sasha positively sniffing the air.

SASHA. Yes, I was. (*He laughs.*)

PLATONOV. You know what it smells of here? Human flesh! And what a delightful smell it is! I feel as if we hadn't seen each other for a hundred years. The winter went on and on forever! And there's my old armchair! Recognise it, Sasha? Six moths ago I was never out of it. Sat there day and night talking to Anna Petrovna about the nature of the world, and losing all the housekeeping at cards.

ANNA PETROVNA. I've been so longing to see you again! I was quite out of patience . . . And you're well?

PLATONOV. Very well . . . But I must tell you one piece of news: you have grown just a shade more beautiful than before.

ANNA PETROVNA. So how have things been?

PLATONOV. Terrible, as usual. Never saw the sky for the whole six months. Ate, drank, slept. And read schoolboy adventure stories aloud to my wife. Terrible!

ANNA PETROVNA. (*to SASHA*) Was it?

SASHA. I thought it was lovely.

PLATONOV. Sasha, it was appalling!

SASHA. It was a little bit dull, naturally.

PLATONOV. It wasn't a little bit dull, my love — it was extremely dull. (*to ANNA PETROVNA*) I was pining for you!

SASHA. You got back yesterday?

ANNA PETROVNA. On the evening train.

PLATONOV. I saw lights here at eleven, but I thought you would be tired out.

ANNA PETROVNA. You should have come in! We sat up talking until two.

PLATONOV. So hot today. And so oppressive.

GLAGOLYEV. I think we may have a storm.

PLATONOV. I'm already starting to pine for the cold again.

COLONEL TRILETZKY. Sashenka, Sashenka! (*He puts a hand on SASHA's arm.*)

DR. TRILETZKY. I thought you were asleep.

COLONEL TRILETZKY. My daughter . . . my son-in-law . . . my son . . . All the great stars of the Colonel Triletzky constellation!

DR. TRILETZKY. If we're not careful he's going to be weeping at the sight of us all. Aren't you, Father?

COLONEL TRILETZKY. Weep? Why should I want to weep?

DR. TRILETZKY. Because you always do! Look at us all! What a family! And think of your grandson!

COLONEL TRILETZKY. (*to SASHA*) Yes, how is the little fellow? Come and see him one of these days.

SASHA. He's well. He sends you his love.

COLONEL TRILETZKY. Really? Amazing child he is! Knows how to send his love to people now, does he?

VOYNITZEV. I think she means metaphorically speaking, colonel.

PLATONOV. He's not one yet, Father-in-law!

DR. TRILETZKY. No, he's always talking about you! He waves his little arms and he pipes: 'Grandpapa! Grandpapa! Where's my grandpapa?'

PLATONOV. He's eleven months old!

DR. TRILETZKY. 'I want to pull my grandpapa's moustache!'

COLONEL TRILETZKY. Good for him! (*He takes out his handkerchief.*) But you're going to get me crying about it!

DR. TRILETZKY. I don't see tears, do I, colonel?

PLATONOV. Stop it now, Kolya.

Dr. Triletzky. All right, so how about Anna Petrovna feeding us instead?

Anna Petrovna. You'll have to wait, doctor, like everybody else.

Dr. Triletzky. She doesn't realise how hungry we are. It's all on the table in there! Caviar, salmon, smoked sturgeon. A great seven-storey pie . . .

Anna Petrovna. How do you know what there is?

Dr. Triletzky. I went and looked! Aren't you hungry, Porfiry Semyonovich? Be absolutely frank, now!

Sasha. (*to DR. TRILETZKY*) You're not all that hungry — you just want to make trouble. You can't bear to see people sitting there in peace.

Dr. Triletzky. I can't bear to see people dying of hunger, Fat Lady.

Platonov. Another flash of quicksilver medical wit.

Anna Petrovna. What a bore the man is! All right, impudence, you wait here and I'll find you something to eat. (*Exit ANNA PETROVNA.*)

Platonov. Though it wouldn't come amiss, now you mention it. I'm rather hungry myself.

(*SOFYA and GREKOVA appear in the garden.*)

Voynitzev. Here are the ladies, anyway. Now we'll put our great scholar to the test!

Platonov. Who is it?

Voynitzev. Aha!

Colonel Triletzky. She's coaxed our little bolter back, by the look of it. (*to PLATONOV*) Took one look at us before and fled!

Platonov. Who are we talking about?

Dr. Triletzky. Oh, yes, and now you're here!

COLONEL TRILETZKY. Come in and go straight out again, I should think!

GLAGOLYEV. May I suggest we pay her no attention?

VOYNITZEV. Just concentrate on the other one, Platonov, and tell us who she is. (*SOFYA ushers GREKOVA in from the garden*)

PLATONOV. *Oh, it's the beetle-juice girl! (GREKOVA stops in her tracks. PLATONOV pays no attention to SOFYA, who watches the scene gravely.)*

DR. TRILETZKY. (*reproachfully*) Misha!

GREKOVA. (*reproachfully*) Misha!

GREKOVA. (*coldly*) Mikhail Vasilyevich.

PLATONOV. (*takes her hand*) Marya Yefimovna! My compliments!

VOYNITZEV. And here is someone else who is longing to meet you, Platonov . . .

PLATONOV. One moment. It's such a pleasure to meet Marya Yefimovna again. (*He tries to kiss her hand.*)

GREKOVA. (*pulls her hand back*) I don't want my hand kissed. Thank you.

PLATONOV. I'm not worthy to kiss you hand, even?

GREKOVA. I've no idea whether you're worthy or not. I just know you don't mean it.

PLATONOV. Don't mean it? What makes you think that?

GREKOVA. You know I don't like it. That's the only reason you do it. It's always the same — you only like doing things that I don't like you doing.

DR. TRILETZKY. Leave her alone, Misha.

PLATONOV. All in good time. (*to GREKOVA*) How are you progressing with your beetle-juice?

GREKOVA. Beetle-juice? What is this about beetle-juice?

PLATONOV. Someone told me you were trying to

make ether out of crushed beetles. Pushing forward the boundaries of science. Admirable!

GREKOVA. You must always make a joke of everything, mustn't you.

DR. TRILETZKY. Always! Of everything!

PLATONOV. I make the doctor my model

VOYNITZEV. Platonov . . .

PLATONOV. But what a charming pink your cheeks are! You're feeling the heat, I can see.

GREKOVA. Why do you keep saying these things to me?

PLATONOV. I'm merely trying to hold a conversation with you. I haven't talked to you for six months or more. Why are you getting so cross about it?

GREKOVA. The sight of me seems to have some strange effect on you. I don't know how I've managed to upset you so. I stay out of your way as far as I possibly can. If Dr. Triletzky hadn't promised me faithfully that you wouldn't be here I shouldn't have come.

DR. TRILETZKY. I said I didn't know whether he'd be here or not.

GREKOVA. (*to DR. TRILETZKY*) You should be ashamed of yourself!

PLATONOV. (*to DR. TRILETZKY*) Absolutely! Deceiving her like that! (*to GREKOVA*) Now you're going to cry, aren't you. All right — have a little cry, then. It can sometimes be a great relief.

(*Exit GREKOVA in tears.*)

DR. TRILETZKY. (*to PLATONOV*) You're such an idiot! One more little incident of that sort and we'll never be friends again!

PLATONOV. What's it to do with you?

Dr. Triletzky. Well, let's suppose—just for the sake of argument—that I happen to be in love with her!

Platonov. Then you'd be grateful to me for the chance to run after her and wipe away her tears.

Dr. Triletzky. I sometimes wonder if you're responsible for your actions! (*Exit DR. TRILETZKY after GREKOVA*)

Sasha. (*reproachfully*) Misha! Please!

Glagolyev. There was a time when we treated women with respect!

Colonel Triletzky. We get her back in, and—bang!—there's her head on the floor all over again!

Platonov. Yes. Stupid of me. Stupidity begets stupidity.

Sofya. And you never could bear stupidity.

Platonov. (*turns to her*) I'm sorry . . .

Sofya. I didn't think you were even going to notice me.

Platonov. I don't believe we've met.

Sofya. You don't recognise me, then?

Voynitzev. (*to PLATONOV*) Careful! This is a serious examination!

Colonel Triletzky. Future career depends on it!

Voynitzev. No? Well, then, may I introduce my wife? Sofya Yegorovna

Platonov. Sofya Yegorovna . . . Your wife?

Sofya. Have I changed so much?

Platonov. No, but . . . here! And you're married? (*to VOYNITZEV*) This is the lady? Why didn't you say?

Voynitzev. A little surprise.

Sofya. Have you forgotten, Platonov?

Voynitzev. A little reminder of your student days.

Sofya. I was hardly out of school.

YOVNITZEV. And this is his wife. Alexandra Ivanovna.

SOFYA. (*to SASHA*) I'm very pleased to meet you.

VOYNITZEV. The colonel's daughter. And the sister of the wittiest man in the world. Apart from Platonov himself.

SOFYA. (*to PLATONOV*) So we're both married?

PLATONOV. I wonder you recognised me. The last five years have ravaged me like rats at a cheese. My life has not turned out as you might have supposed.

VOYNITZEV. She thought you were the second Byron!

COLONEL TRILETZKY. We all thought he was another Newton!

SOFYA. And in fact you're the village schoolmaster?

PLATONOV. Yes.

SOFYA. The village schoolmaster. I find that difficult to believe. Why haven't you . . . done better?

PLATONOV. Why haven't I done better?

VOYNITZEV. (*to PLATONOV*) Now *you're* being called to account!

COLONEL TRILETZKY. This makes a change!

PLATONOV. Why haven't I done better? What can I say?

SOFYA. You finished university, at any rate?

VOYNITZEV. No, he gave it up.

COLONEL TRILETZKY. He knew it all. Nothing more they could teach him.

PLATONOV. I got married.

SOFYA. I see. Still, that doesn't stop you leading a descent life, does it?

PLATONOV. A decent life?

COLONEL TRILETZKY. The boot's on the other foot now, and no mistake!

SOFYA. Perhaps I shouldn't have put it like that. But giving up university doesn't stop you doing something worthwhile, does it? It doesn't stop you fighting for political freedom or the emancipation of women? It doesn't stop you serving a cause?

PLATONOV. Oh, dear. What can I say to that?

GLAGOLYEV. I think our Savonarola has met his match!

COLONEL TRILETZKY. Come on, Misha! Return her fire!

PLATONOV. No, she's right. There's nothing to stop me. The question is whether there was ever anything there to be stopped. I wasn't put into this world to do things; I was put here to prevent others from doing them. (*PETRIN appears in the garden.*) To lie here like some great flat stone and trip them up. To make them stub their toes against me.

SOFYA. And shall you lie in the same place for the rest of your life?

PLATONOV. (*indicates PETRIN*) Who's going to hinder people like him, for instance, if I don't do it? Look at him! Anna Petrovna hasn't been back for a day, and already he's round here dunning her.

VOYNITZEV. Platonov—please! Don't start, I beg of you. We went through all this last summer. (*PETRIN comes on to the verandah.*) Gerasim Kuzmich! (*They shake hands.*)

PLATONOV. You were deep in thought out there. What were you contemplating? Life and death? Or bills and promissory notes?

VOYNITZEV. (*to PETRIN*) And this is my wife. Sofya Yegorovna.

PETRIN. (*to PLATONOV*) Don't talk to me about bills. (*He shakes hands with SOFYA.*) How do you do?

(*to PLATONOV*) Don't talk to me about promissory notes! (*to VOYNITZEV*) Yes, of course. Congratulations! (*to PLATONOV*) They're nothing but dreams and delusions, my friend! They say: 'You possess money!' Put when you reach out your hand for the money you possess, you find you possess nothing.

PLATONOV. (*to SOFYA*) The old general didn't know what he was doing at the end of his life.

PETRIN. Yes, and who was there to help him?

PLATONOV. He didn't know what he was signing.

PETRIN. Who sat with him to the last and closed his eyes?

PLATONOV. (*to SOFYA*) You wonder at me. And rightly so. But there's a whole world for you to wonder at here! A whole new world of fools and knaves.

VOYNITZEV. Now, Platonov . . .

PLATONOV. Sixty taverns, this fine gentleman owns.

PETRIN. Sixty-three.

PLATONOV. I beg your pardon.

PETRIN. And I should think you've drunk in all of them, haven't you?

PLATONOV. A public benefactor. Someone we all touch our caps to.

PETRIN. I am also a member of a learned profession. I am a qualified lawyer! Did you know that? On top of which I'm in the seventh grade of the civil service. And I have lived a little longer than you!

VOYNITZEV. Please!

GLAGOLYEV. No, but it's true! Some of us have lived a little longer than others!

PLATONOV. Wonderful. And what does that prove?

PETRIN. When you get to my age you'll find out!

GLAGOLYEV. (*to PLATONOV*) You never knew the past, you see.

PETRIN. To survive your life — that takes some doing!

GLAGOLYEV. (*agreeing*) We knew how to enjoy our life!

PETRIN. But there's a price to be paid!

PLATONOV. (*to SOFYA*) Look at him, though! They all bend the knee before this jumped-up nobody. And why? Because they're all up to their ears in debt to him!

VOYNITZEV. Now that's enough, Platonov! It's very awkward for the hosts when guests fall out.

PLATONOV. (*to SOFYA*) Are you embarrassed by our rural entertainments?

SOFYA. I find it all very illuminating.

VOYNITZEV. (*to PLATONOV*) Sometimes you go too far, though.

PETRIN. What have I ever done to him?

PLATONOV. But that's the worst thing of all — that even those with some pretension to honour will say nothing! They all maintain this silence, this deathly silence! (*COLONEL TRILETZKY snores in his sleep.*)

SASHA. (*shakes him*) Wake up, Papa! You can't go to sleep here!

COLONEL TRILETZKY. Lunch?

PLATONOV. No. Go back to sleep again.

SASHA. Misha!

(*OSIP appears in the garden, waiting awkwardly.*)

PLATONOV. I prefer the company of good honest criminals. (*He calls:*) Osip!

VOYNITZEV. Oh, no!

GLAGOLYEV. Not him again!

PETRIN. What's he going to do — invite him in?

PLATONOV. Come in, Osip. (*OSIP comes on to the verandah, very out of place. He is concealing something under his shirt.* (*to SOFYA*:) May I introduce my friend Osip?

VOYNITZEV. (*resignedly*) Wipe your boots then, Osip.

PLATONOV. Osip is our local horsethief.

VOYNITZEV. What are you doing here, Osip?

OSIP. Nothing, sir. Waiting for the mistress. Say welcome home, like.

VOYNITZEV. Very thoughtful of you, Osip. (*to SOFYA*) All part of your introduction to local society, I suppose.

COLONEL TRILETZKY. Lives rough, this one.

GLAGOLYEV. In the forest.

PETRIN. Like a wide animal.

PLATONOV. Our local burglar. And murderer. Aren't you, Osip?

OSIP. (*to VOYNITZEV*) Came to say congratulations, hope you'll be very happy, sir.

VOYNITZEV. Thank you, Osip.

PLATONOV. Look at that grin! There's a ton of iron in that face!

VOYNITZEV. So what have you been stealing off us this winter, Osip?

OSIP. Haven't been stealing nothing sir.

VOYNITZEV. No?

OSIP. No, sir. Been away, sir.

VOYNITZEV. Where have you been, Osip?

OSIP. Been in prison, sir.

PLATONOV. Why have you been in prison?

OSIP. Because it's cold in the forest in winter.

PETRIN. Prison! Why have they never packed you off to Siberia for good and all? Look, he's got something hidden under his shirt even now!

VOYNITZEV. What is it, Osip?

OSIP. Nothing sir.

PLATONOV. Nothing, he says! And nothing is what we do about it! That's why he doesn't go to Siberia! We all know he's a thief—but we all know he's a murderer, too, so no one's got the courage to look inside his shirt. And that's all that stops the rest of them here from going to Siberia! They're all standing here with a bulging wad of nothing stuffed away in their shirts, and no one's got the courage to challenge them!

VOYNITZEV. Platonov, really!

GLAGOLYEV. He's gone too far this time! There is a limit to everything, and he has gone beyond it!

PLATONOV. Sixty-three taverns, this man owns! (*to OSIP*) I don't suppose you've got sixty-three kopecks. You're only a beginner at thieving!

PETRIN. Are you seriously comparing me with a common horsethief?

PLATONOV. Certainly not! I wouldn't insult horse-thieves! (*Uproar, through which COLONEL TRI-LETZKY sleeps.*)

VOYNITZEV. Please! Please!

PETRIN. (*pointing at PLATONOV*) Either he goes or I go!

VOYNITZEV. (*to OSIP*) *You* go! You're the cause of all this!

PLATONOV. (*pointing at OSIP*) If he goes, I go!

SASHA. (*to PLATONOV*) For the love of God! You're shaming me in front of everyone!

(*Enter ANNA PETROVNA.*)

ANNA PETROVNA. Stop it! Stop it! It's getting like last year all over again! I won't have it! Platonov, we were all perfectly happy until you arrived!

PLATONOV. (*offended*) Oh, you're on their side, are

you? You don't want me here, either? In that case I'll go! (*PLATONOV goes out into the garden.*)

SASHA. (*to ANNA PETROVNA*) I'm so sorry!

ANNA PETROVNA. (*to SASHA*) Don't be silly. He'll calm down in a moment. Osip, what are you doing here?

OSIP. Nothing. Say welcome home, like. Brought you a little baby owl. (*He produces it from inside his shirt.*)

ANNA PETROVNA. Oh, how sweet. Take it round to the stables and find a box for it. Then go to the kitchen door and they'll give you something to eat. (*OSIP goes out into the garden.*) In fact we can all eat. Lunch is served!

SASHA. (*to ANNA PETROVNA*) Please forgive him!

ANNA PETROVNA. There's nothing to forgive! It's all over. It's all forgotten.

GLAGOLYEV. We all know what Platonov's like.

VOYNITZEV. (*to SOFYA*) Yes, there's your Platonov for you, my love!

SOFYA. I'm afraid I upset him. I shouldn't have spoken so frankly.

GLAGOLYEV. No, no, the man's a crank. (*to SASHA*) Saving your presence. (*to SOFYA*) There's no telling what will make him fly up next.

PETRIN. It's like having a performing bear in the house. Will he perform, or will he maul you?

ANNA PETROVNA. Gerasim Kuzmich. I haven't said hello to you.

PETRIN. Anna Petrovna! Could I have a word with you?

ANNA PETROVNA. You'll stay to lunch?

PETRIN. Yet, but if I could just have one word first . . .

ANNA PETROVNA. Where's our performing bear hiding himself now? (*to the others*) Do go on in to lunch!

(*ANNA PETROVNA goes towards the garden, followed by PETRIN.*)

PETRIN. If you could just give me some hope . . .

ANNA PETROVNA. After lunch! There's always more hope after lunch. (*ANNA PETROVNA goes out into the garden.*)

SASHA. (*despairingly*) Father! Please!

COLONEL TRILETZKY. (*wakes with a start*) Haven't had lunch, have we?

VOYNITZEV. Come on, Colonel . . . (*VOYNITZEV helps COLONEL TRILETZKY out. GLAGOLYEV begins to user SOFYA and SASHA out after him.*)

SASHA. I'm sorry. I'm sorry.

GLAGOLYEV. No, no! What should we do without the colonel and his family to entertain us! (*Exeunt SOFYA and SASHA. GLAGOLYEV is detained by PETRIN.*)

PETRIN. Just tell me. Did you?

GLAGOLYEV. Did I what?

PETRIN. Did you ask her?

GLAGOLYEV. Not yet.

PETRIN. My dear fellow! What are you waiting for? The colonel will get in ahead of you!

GLAGOLYEV. The colonel? The colonel hasn't got two kopecks for a candle!

PETRIN. He's got kopecks enough to buy skyrockets for her! Behind the old summerhouse — Yakov showed me. Might say more to a woman than flowers! You do want to marry her?

GLAGOLYEV. I'm not averse to the idea.

PETRIN. Well, then.

GLAGOLYEV. But will *she* want to marry *me*? That could be the difficulty, you see.

PETRIN. Of course she will!

GLAGOLYEV. Will she? Which of us knows the secrets of another's heart?

PETRIN. Lovely woman — handsome man. You're made for each other! Shall I ask her for you?

GLAGOLYEV. I can do my own courting, thank you! What's it to do with you?

PETRIN. A man needs a wife, Porfiry Semyonovich! An estate needs a man! And debts need someone to pay them! I don't want to take her to court and force her to sell up! I'm a reasonable man, Porfiry Semyonovich! All I want is my money! (*ANNA PETROVNA appears in the garden, her arm in PLATONOV's.*) Here she is, Porfiry Semyonovich! Ask her now!

GLAGOLYEV. (*hesitates*) I can't do it on an empty stomach. Lunch first!

PETRIN. Your happiness — that's all I want! Your happiness and my money. (*Exeunt GLAGOLYEV and PETRIN in the direction of lunch. Enter ANNA PE-TROVNA and PLATONOV from the garden.*)

ANNA PETROVNA. But I *can't* get rid of them, you see. Nor can you, for all your eloquence. I depend upon them! It's like a very complicated position on a chess board. If I didn't make Porfiry Semyonovich just a little bit jealous of the colonel . . . if I didn't make the colonel just a little bit jealous of the doctor . . . if I wasn't protected from the doctor by poor little Grekova . . . if our good tavernkeeper didn't believe he'd get his money from our great lover of women . . . if you weren't here to lighten my heart . . . why, then the queen would fall. I should lose the estate, Platonov! I should lose everything. Then what would you do? Any of you? The lion must roar — of course he must — but a little more softly, Platonov, or he'll roar the whole house down. Yes? Now you wait here. I'm going to send Marya Yefimovna out to you. I found *her* in tears, Platonov! So you're going to give her your paw and apologise.

(*Enter VOYNITZEV.*)

VOYNITZEV. Come on! They're all waiting to drink our health!

ANNA PETROVNA. He's got something else to do first. (*to PLATONOV*) Now, wait! Don't you dare come into lunch until you've done as I told you! (*Exit ANNA PETROVNA*)

VOYNITZEV. What's all this?

PLATONOV. I'm offering my paw to get my lunch . . . Sergey, you're a luck man. She's a lovely woman, your Sofya. Are you happy?

VOYNITZEV. I don't know . . .

PLATONOV. You don't know?

VOYNITZEV. Are you and Sasha happy?

PLATONOV. We're a family! We've made a nest! One of these days you'll understand what that means. Take Sasha away from me and I think I should be finished. Utterly destroyed. We're the perfect couple—she's a fool and I'm a rogue. *Aren't* you happy?

VOYNITZEV. I suppose we are. I suppose this is what being happy is.

(*Enter DR. TRILETZKY, eating, glass in one hand, bottle in the other.*)

PLATONOV. (*to DR. TRILETZKY*) You've been stuffing yourself already, then. Have you forgiven me?

DR. TRILETZKY. What for? Come on! We've got to drink to the great homecoming. (*He puts his arm round PLATONOV.*) Drink, drink, drink!

PLATONOV. Have you seen your patients today?

DR. TRILETZKY. (*moves away from him*) Misha, once and for all, if you're going to lecture me, let's make a regular arrangement. Private moral coaching, an hour a day, four to five, and I'll pay you a ruble a time!

VOYNITZEV. (*puts his arm round both of them*) Come on, my friends, let's go and drink together! Then fate can do its worst. To hell with moneylenders, to hell with creditors! Just so long as all the people I love in this world are alive and well. You're all I have!

DR. TRILETZKY. We're all we all have!

(*Enter GREKOVA. She stops at the sight of them.*)

PLATONOV. Come on! I'm going to drink to everything, with everything there is to drink! I haven't been drunk for a long, long time, and I'm going to get drunk today! (*They start to go, but stop at the sight of GRE-KOVA.*) Marya Yefimovna! I apologise. I publicly beg your forgiveness. I burn with shame. Give me your hand . . . I go down on one knee and publicly kiss your hand! (*GREKOVA snatches her hand back.*) And now she's going to start snivelling again! (*Exit GREKOVA in tears.*) Come back here, Beetle-juice! (*Exit PLATONOV after her.*)

DR. TRILETZKY. Misha, I implore you!

VOYNITZEV. Can you *never* be serious? (*Exeunt DR. TRILETZKY and VOYNITZEV after him. Curtain, as a cheerful dance is stuck up offstage.*)

Scene Two

*The garden. As in the previous scene, less the verandah.
The music continues softly offstage. Enter SASHA,
carrying something under a napkin.*

SASHA. (*calls, softly*) Where are you? Are you there?

(*OSIP emerges from the trees. SASHA takes the napkin
off what she is holding; it is a plate of food.*)

OSIP. We're both of us thieves, then. (*He takes the
plate, sits down, and eats hungrily with his fingers.*)
SASHA. Take your cap off. It's a sin to eat with your
head covered. And you say a little grace, now! (*OSIP
removes his cap, and continues to eat. There is the distant
whistle of a train.*) There—that's the evening train. It'll
be dark soon. And they still haven't finished lunch! Eating, drinking. Sinking, dancing. Then eating and drinking again. My head's ringing . . . And they couldn't
find a few scraps in the kitchen for you . . . ? Well, God
be with them . . . As soon as it's dark we'll be having
the fireworks. I haven't seen fireworks since I was a girl.
(*Another train whistle, a little nearer, and then for a moment the faint sound of the locomotive.*) There it goes.
Over the crossing. Past our little house . . . (*Pause.
OSIP hands the plate back to SASHA and wipes his
mouth.*)
OSIP. I kissed her once.
SASHA. Anna Petrovna? You kissed her? (*She sits
beside him.*)
OSIP. Hot summer's day. Like today. In the forest
here. I'm going along this track and I look round and
there she is, she's standing in a little stream and she's

holding her dress up with one hand and she's scooping up water in a dock leaf with the other. She scoops. She drinks. Scoops. Drinks. Scoops again, and pours it over her head. It's one of those days when you can feel the air heavy on you, and you can't hear nothing but the buzzing of the flies . . . She pays no heed to me. Just another peasant, she thinks. So I go down to the edge of the stream, right close up to her, as close as I am to you now, and I just look at her. Like this, like I'm looking at you. And she stands there in the water in front of me, with her skirts up in her hand, and she bends, she scoops, she pours. And the water runs over her hair, over her face and her neck, then down over her dress, and all she says is: 'What are you staring at, idiot? Haven't you ever seen a human being before?' And she scoops and she pours, and I just stand gazing. Then suddenly she turns and gives me a sharp look. 'Oh,' she says, 'you've taken a fancy to me, have you?' And I say: 'I reckon I could kiss you and die.' So that made her laugh. 'All right,' she says, 'you can kiss me if you like.' Well, I felt as if I'd been thrown into a furnace. I went up to her—into the stream, boots and all, I didn't think twice—and I took her by the shoulder, very lightly, and I kissed her right here, on her cheek, and here on her neck, as hard as ever I could.

SASHA. So what did she do then?

OSIP. 'Now, then,' she says, 'be off with you! And you wash a little more often,' she says, 'and you do something about your nails!' And off I went.

SASHA. She's a bold one, all right.

OSIP. After that you'd have thought I'd gone mad. Couldn't eat. Couldn't sleep. Everywhere I went I could see her in front of me. Shut my eyes—there she was again. I must have looked right soft. I wanted to go round and shoot the poor old general! And then when she was widowed I started doing all kinds of little things for her. Shot partridges for her — caught quails — painted that old summerhouse of hers all different colours. Took her a live wolf once. She's only to say and I'd do it. Tell me to eat myself and I'd eat myself . . .

(*ANNA PETROVNA appears among the trees in the background. She moves irresolutely first in this direction and then in that, looking for someone.*)

SASHA. There she is . . . She'll see you.

OSIP. Why should I care?

SASH. It's true, though. When you're soft on someone there's nothing to be done with you. When I first loved Platonov and still didn't know that he loved me I went through terrible torments. Wandered about the forest like a lost soul.

OSIP. And now what does he do? He dangles round her ladyship! Not much heart, that husband of yours. Got the brains, though, and he's got the words. He could have the whole female race after him if he wanted.

SASHA. That's enough now. I don't like that kind of talk.

VOYNITZEV. (*calls, off*) Sofya! Sofya!

DR. TRILETZKY. (*calls, off*) Misha! Where are you? (*ANNA PETROVNA vanishes.*)

SASHA. Now they're all coming out. They'll find you, for sure. Anyway, it's no good sitting here moping after her. That won't get you anywhere.

OSIP. Why should he want more women after him, though? He's got the best of them already

(*OSIP melts away beneath the trees as VOYNITZEV enters.*)

SASHA. Is it time for the fireworks?

VOYNITZEV. Yes, but I've lost Sofya.

SASHA. I'll fetch Platonov. You won't start without us, will you?

VOYNITZEV. I thought she was in the garden. (*Enter DR. TRILETZKY, noticeably drunk.*) Have you seen Sofya?

DR. TRILETZKY. No. Looking for Misha.

VOYNITZEV. (*calls*) Sofya . . . ! (*Exit VOYNITZEV.*)

DR. TRILETZKY. (*calls*) Misha! (*to SASHA*) I've got a ruble for him! Have a ruble, Sasha . . . (*He sees the empty plate in her hand.*) Poor Sasha! Eating out here on your own! Have two rubles, Sasha! Have three!

SASHA. (*brushes the money aside*) Oh, no! Are you as drunk as that?

DR. TRILETZKY. I'm not drunk, Sasha! It's Gerasim Kuzmich who's drunk! Gave me all his money to look after! 'If I don't give this to you,' he said, 'I know I'll go and give it to someone else.' (*He sniffs the money.*) Peasant money . . . Here — four rubles for my lovely sister. And if you think I'm drunk you want to see Father!

SASHA. What have I done to deserve this? Where is he?

DR. TRILETZKY. Behind the sofa.

SASHA. No use expecting any help from you, I suppose. Where's Misha?

DR. TRILETZKY. I can't find him!

SASHA. Well, find him! I'll find Father. (*Exit SASHA.*)

DR. TRILETZKY. (*calls*) Misha! Misha!

(*Exit DR. TRILETZKY. Enter SOFYA from under the trees. She sits down on one of the garden seats.*)

VOYNITZEV. (*calls, off*) Sofya! Where are you?

Dr. Triletzky. (*calls, off*) A reward of one ruble for anyone who finds Platonov!

(*Enter PLATONOV from the same direction as SOFYA.*)

Platonov. I follow you into the living-room — you go back into the dining-room. I go into the dining-room — you go into the garden. I come into the garden — you run back towards the house.

Sofya. You keep talking about the past. What does it matter? A student loved a schoolgirl; a schoolgirl loved a student. It's an old story! Old and trite! Too old and trite for it to mean much to us now.

Platonov. Then what are you so frightened of?

Sofya. I'm not frightened of anything!

Platonov. Is every man you meet really such a threat to your Sergey? If I've talked to you too much this evening, if I've wearied you with my attentions, then it's because you're an intelligent and sympathetic woman. What do you think? That I want to take you away from your husband? That I'm in love with you? That you've somehow made a conquest of the local intellectual? Tamed the village eccentric? How wonderful! What bliss! What a nice box of chocolates for our little egotist!

Sofya. You've gone mad.

Platonov. Run away, then! Run back to him! No one's forcing you to stay here! (*pause*) So hot, even now . . . I shouldn't have drunk so much . . . (*pause*) Why haven't I done better? The first thing you asked me! Not 'Are you well?' or 'Are you happy?' Not at all! 'Why haven't you done better?'

Sofya. I'm sorry.

Platonov. No, you're right. Why haven't I? Teeming

evil all around me, fouling the earth, swallowing up my
brothers in Christ, while I sit here with folded hands. I
shall be the same when I'm forty, the same when I'm
fifty. I shan't change now. Not until I decline into shuf-
fling old age, and stupefied indifference to everything
outside my own body. A wasted life! Then death. And
when I think of that death I'm terrified. (*pause*) Why
haven't I done better? I might ask the same of you.
What's happened to that pure heart you used to have?
Where's the old sincerity, the truthfulness, the boldness?
You ask me why I haven't done better; do you ever ask
your husband? (*SOFYA gets to her feet. PLATONOV
makes her sit down again.*) One last word, and then I'll
let you go. You were so splendid once! No, let me finish . . . You were good. You had greatness in you. (*He
takes her hand.*) What in all the wide world made you
marry that man?

SOFYA. Sergey? He's a fine man!

PLATONOV. He's a moral pygmy!

SOFYA. He's my husband!

PLATONOV. He's bogged down in debt — he's helpless
with doing nothing!

SOFYA. Lower your voice, will you! There are people
about!

PLATONOV. I don't care! Let them all hear! (*Quietly:*)
I'm sorry if I spoke sharply. I loved you, though. Loved
you more than all the world. This hair. These hands. This
face . . . And what can you do here? You'll only go
deeper and deeper into the mire. Why do we never lead
the life we have it in us to lead? If I had the strength I
should uproot us from this mudhole — uproot us both!
We'd leave! Tonight! Take the night train and never
return!

SOFYA. What are you saying?

PLATONOV. You know what I'm saying . . .

(*Enter PETRIN and GLAGOLYEV, both a little bit drunk.*)

PETRIN. (*to GLAGOLYEV*) Put a ruble in front of me and I'll steal it! (*SOFYA flees into the depths of the garden.*)

PLATONOV. Sofya! (*He runs after her.*)

PETRIN. I should, Porfiry! I'd steal it! I honestly should! If I thought I could get away with it! Put a ruble in front of *you* and you'd steal it!

GLAGOLYEV. I shouldn't, Gerasya! I shouldn't, you know!

PETRIN. Show me an honest man, Porfiry, and I'll show you a fool!

GLAGOLYEV. I'm a fool, Gerasya!

PETRIN. (*sadly*) Yes. You're a fool. And it's no good just sitting in there and staring at her! What kind of way is that to win a woman? You were just sitting there like a mushroom!

GLAGOLYEV. I'll win her, Gerasya never you fear! I'll marry her yet!

PETRIN. Yes, but when, Porfiry, when? Who knows how long we've got, at our age? Ask her tonight. Porfiry! It's a beautiful summer's night. And she's in love! Didn't you see her laughing at lunch? Didn't you see the wild look in her eye? Here she comes. Look at her! Look at her! (*Enter ANNA PETROVNA and GREKOVA, in the depths of the garden.*) She's followed you out here.

GLAGOLYEV. She's got Marya Yefimovna with her.

ANNA PETROVNA. (*calls*) Doctor! Doctor?

PETRIN. She's trying to get rid of her. She wants to be alone.

Dr. Triletzky. (*calls, off*) Misha! Where are you, Misha? (*ANNA PETROVNA urges GREKOVA off in the direction of the voice.*)

Petrin. You see? She's waiting for you! Quick! Before the colonel comes out! One more glass to get his courage up and he'll go into battle! You'll never have another chance like this! (*ANNA PETROVNA, now that GRE-KOVA is out of sight, goes off purposefully in another direction.*) After her, then, Porfiry! Steal that ruble!

(*Exit GLAGOLYEV uncertainly after ANNA PE-TROVNA. Enter VOYNITZEV.*)

Voynitzev. I've lost Sofya. I can't understand it . . . (*He looks off in the direction taken by ANNA PETROVNA.*) That isn't her, is it?

Petrin. No, no! That way, that way!

(*He directs VOYNITZEV in some other direction, then goes off anxiously after GLAGOLYEV. Enter GREKOVA*

Grekova. (*to VOYNITZEV*) Platonov?. Voynitzev
Sofya?. Grekova
I'm sorry.. Voynitzev
I beg your pardon.

(*Exit GREKOVA, in some confusion. Enter SOFYA, in some agitation..*)

Sofya. Sergey!
Voynitzev. Sofya! I thought I'd lost you forever! Where have you been?
Sofya. Let's go away from here!

VOYNITZEV. Away?

SOFYA. Anywhere! Abroad!

VOYNITZEV. If you like.

SOFYA. Now!

VOYNITZEV. Now?

SOFYA. Tonight.

VOYNITZEV. Sofya!

SOFYA. Please Sergey!

VOYNITZEV. But . . . but . . . what about the fireworks!

SOFYA. No — no fireworks!

VOYNITZEV. Sofya, my love, I know how dull it is for you here . . .

SOFYA. There's a train. There's a night train.

VOYNITZEV. My love, we're not *that* boring! Not all of us, anyway. I'm sure it would help if you talked to Platonov.

SOFYA. Platonov?

(*Enter PLATONOV at the sound of his name. He stops at the sight of VOYNITZEV, and stands at the edge of the trees, unnoticed, watching them.*)

VOYNITZEV. I know you're disappointed in him, I saw you avoiding him all afternoon. And he has become a bit of a bear, I admit. But he's not like the others. He's someone I love. He's someone you'll love, too, when you know him a little better. Come on, let's find him!

SOFYA. Sergey, please listen . . .

VOYNITZEV. No, no — you listen to Platonov. I know he'll persuade you to stay! At least until we've had the fireworks!

(*Exeunt VOYNITZEV and SOFYA. PLATONOV goes to follow them. Enter ANNA PETROVNA.*)

ANNA PETROVNA. And here he is. Our philosopher. Shunning us all. Pacing the garden and thinking his own thoughts. But what a perfect summer's night! Cool air at last. And the first star . . . What a pity ladies aren't supposed to sleep outside under the open sky. When I was a little girl I always slept in the garden in summer. (*pause*) You've got a new tie.

PLATONOV. Yes.

ANNA PETROVNA. I'm in such an odd mood today . . . I feel pleased with everything . . . Say something, Platonov!

PLATONOV. What do you want me to say?

ANNA PETROVNA. I want to hear the sound of your voice. I want to hear it saying—I don't know—something new, something sharp, something sweet. Because you're being terribly clever today, and you're looking terribly handsome, and I'm more in love with you than ever. And you're being so nice! You're causing scarcely any trouble at all!

PLATONOV. I've never seen you looking more lovely.

ANNA PETROVNA. Are we friends, Platonov?

PLATONOV. Of course. If we're not friends, who is?

ANNA PETROVNA. Real friends? Great friends?

PLATONOV. What is this? We're friends, we're friends! You're behaving like a schoolgirl!

ANNA PETROVNA. So, we're friends. But you know, do you, my dear sir, that from friendship between a man and a woman it's only a short step to love?

PLATONOV. It is indeed? You and I shall not be taking that one step to perdition, however short it may be.

ANNA PETROVNA. So you see love as perdition, do you? I see it as something noble. Why should we be ashamed of it? Why shouldn't we take that one short step?

PLATONOV. (*stares at her*) Let's go inside and dance, shall we?

ANNA PETROVNA. You can't dance! I think it's time you and I had a little talk. I don't know quite where to begin, though. You're such a difficult man! Now try to listen for once, and not to philosophise . . . (*She sits.*) Sit down . . . Look, he's quite embarrassed! It's all right, my dear—your wife can't hear us!

PLATONOV. Perhaps I should say something first.

ANNA PETROVNA. Perhaps you should.

PLATONOV. It's not worth it. I promise you, Anna Petrovna—it's simply not worth it.

ANNA PETROVNA. Isn't it? Now you listen to me. Sit down . . . Sit down! (*He sits beside her.*) Look, if you were free, I shouldn't think twice—I'd make myself your wife. I'd bestow my rank and station on you. But as it is . . . (*pause*) Am I to take your silence as a sign of agreement? (*pause*) I think in the circumstances it is a little ungentlemanly of you not to say *something*.

PLATONOV. (*jumps to his feet*) Let's forget this conversation! Let's pretend it never took place!

ANNA PETROVNA. You are a clown, Misha.

PLATONOV. I respect you! And I respect in myself the respect I have for you! I'm not against harmless diversion . . .

ANNA PETROVNA. I know, Platonov.

PLATONOV. But not with a beautiful, intelligent, untrammelled woman like you! What—a month or two of foolishness, and then to go our ways in shame? I couldn't do it!

ANNA PETROVNA. I wasn't talking about foolishness. I was talking about love.

PLATONOV. And do you think I don't love you? I love you for your goodness, for your generous heart. I love you desperately — I love you to distraction! I'll lay down my life for you, if that's what you want! Does every love have to be reduced to the same common denominator? I love you as a woman, yes, but I also love you as a person. On top of which, my dear, I am just a tiny bit married.

ANNA PETROVNA. (*rises*) You've also had just a tiny bit too much to drink, and you're being just a tiny bit hypocritical. Go on, then. When your head's clear we'll have another talk.

PLATONOV. No, the trouble is, I have true feelings for you, and you know it. (*quietly and intimately*) If only it were a game, my precious, I should long since have been your lover. (*Exit PLATONOV.*)

ANNA PETROVNA. (*to herself*) Intolerable man! (*She calls.*) Come back here! Misha! Misha! . . .

(*She is about to run after him when GLAGOLYEV enters suddenly from among the trees.*)

GLAGOLYEV. Anna Petrovna!

ANNA PETROVNA. Oh! You quite startled me!

GLAGOLYEV. Anna Petrovna, you know, I believe, in what high regard I hold your sex. I have more than once been accused of romanticism, but for me a world without women would be akin to a paradise without angels. And yet such is the world, during the winter months at any rate, in which I myself live. Anna Petrovna . . .

COLONEL TRILETZKY. (*calls, off*) Anna Petrovna!

ANNA PETROVNA. I'm afraid we've been spotted by the artillery.

GLAGOLYEV. (*turns to look at COLONEL TRI-LETZKY*) Yes. I'll come straight to the point, then (*Exit ANNA PETROVNA.*) Anna Petrovna, will you be the angel in my paradise?

COLONEL TRILETZKY. (*off*) You're getting my feet all muddled up! Perfectly all right on my own! (*GLAGOLYEV turns to watch COLONEL TRILETZKY. Exit ANNA PETROVNA in the opposite direction.*)

GLAGOLYEV. (*becomes aware the ANNA PETROVNA has departed*) Anna Petrovna!

(*Enter PETRIN from behind the trees.*)

PETRIN. That way! (*Exit GLAGOLYEV after ANNA PETROVNA, and PETRIN after GLAGOLYEV.*)

(*Enter COLONEL TRILETZKY, drunk, attended by DR. TRILETZKY and SASHA. Dr. TRILETZKY, who is wearing the officer's peaked cap in which his father arrived, is amused by the colonel's condition.*)

COLONEL TRILETZKY. Don't push me! Don't push me! (*He discovers he is not being pushed.*) Oh, you're there.

SASHA. If you've no fear before God you might at least have some shame in front of other people! Everyone staring at you! Everyone laughing at you! (*to DR. TRILETZKY*) It's nothing to laugh about!

DR. TRILETZKY. Where's Misha, though?

COLONEL TRILETZKY. Where's Anna Petrovna?

SASHA. Vanished at the sight of you, of course.

COLONEL TRILETZKY. Something I wanted to ask her.

DR. TRILETZKY. He's forgotten what it was!

SASHA. It's not funny, Kolya!

COLONEL TRILETZKY. What was I saying?

DR. TRILETZKY. You could had been a general.

SASHA. Don't encourage him!

COLONEL TRILETZKY. Yes! Another five years or so, and I could have been a general! If I'd been five years older when I reached retiring age . . . No, if I'd been five years younger when I was born . . . What do I mean?

SASHA. Come on — home. You shouldn't be allowed inside a decent house. You're an old man! You should be setting the others an example!

COLONEL TRILETZKY. You're just like your mother! Do you know that? Day and night she used to go on. This isn't right, that isn't right . . . Just like your poor old dear departed mother, my pet! Same eyes, same hair. Some way of waddling like a goose . . . (*He kisses her.*) God, how I loved her!

SASHA. That's enough, now. Come on!

COLONEL TRILETZKY. I will, my love. Whatever you say. I haven't always been a good man, Sasha. But I loved your mother. And I never took money from anyone.

DR. TRILETZKY. Have another ruble. (*He gives him one.*)

COLONEL TRILETZKY. (*takes the money*) All I had to do was to dip my hand in with the rest of them and I could have been rich and famous . . . I could have been a general!

SASHA. Kolya, give him his hat back before he catches cold. Tell Misha I've gone, when you find him.

DR. TRILETZKY. What about the fireworks?

SASHA. I'll just have to wait for another time.

COLONEL TRILETZKY. Right, then, quick march . . . ! I'll tell you what. I'll carry you.

SASHA. Don't be silly.

COLONEL TRILETZKY. I'll carry you! Always used to carry your mother. Couldn't walk straight myself — still pick her up and carry her! Come on!

SASHA. Certainly not. Put your cap on properly. (*She straightens his cap for him.*) Smarten you up a bit.

COLONEL TRILETZKY. We rolled all the way down a

hill together once. Never said a word about it, poor love. Just laughed, bless her.

(*Exit COLONEL TRILETZKY, supported by SASHA. Enter VOYNITZEV.*)

VOYNITZEV. Where's Platonov? I can't find him anywhere.

DR. TRILETZKY. Nor can I. Have another ruble instead. Is it the fireworks?

VOYNITZEV. There won't be any fireworks if I can't find Flatonov.

DR. TRILETZKY. Won't be any . . . ? (*He calls.*) Misha!

VOYNITZEV. (*calls*) Misha!

DR. TRILETZKY. (*calls*) Misha!

(*Exeunt VOYNITZEV and DR. TRILETZKY. Enter PLATONOV and SOFYA.*)

PLATONOV. Going?

SOFYA. Tonight.

PLATONOV. Forever?

SOFYA. Forever.

PLATONOV. What did you tell Sergey?

SOFYA. Nothing.

PLATONOV. What did he say?

SOFYA. He told me to talk to you.

PLATONOV. To *me*?

SOFYA. He said you'd persuade me to stay. (*Pause. They look at each other.*)

PLATONOV. Go.

SOFYA. Go?

PLATONOV. Tonight. At once. You're right — it's the only way. Otherwise I can't answer for the consequences.

(*Pause. They stand looking at each other. Enter GREKOVA.*)

GREKOVA. Platonov . . . (*She stops at the sight of SOFYA. But SOFYA suddenly turns and flees.*) I'm sorry. But I can't bear this any longer. You seem to be following me! Everywhere I go — there you are! *Are* you following me?

PLATONOV. Beetle-juice! Come here, you lovely creature!

GREKOVA. What? (*She crosses to him nervously.*)

PLATONOV. You weird and wonderful woman! (*He kisses her.*)

GREKOVA. Why are you kissing me?

PLATONOV. I've got to kiss someone!

GREKOVA. Do you . . . do you love me, then?

PLATONOV. Why, do you love me, you foolish head-strong woman?

GREKOVA. I don't know. That depends on whether you . . . (*He kisses her.*) You shouldn't do that if you don't. (*He kisses her.*) *Do* you love me?

PLATONOV. Not at all, my precious! That's why I'm kissing you! (*She bursts into tears, flees, and runs into DR. TRILETZKY.*)

DR. TRILETZKY. And here he is! The man everyone wants to see!

GREKOVA. *I* never want to see him again! And if you have any respect for me at all — if you have any respect for yourself — you'll never see him again, either.

DR. TRILETZKY. But he's my brother-in-law!

GREKOVA. Yes, everything's a joke to you, too, isn't it. Well, you joke away together, then. That's all you can ever do!

DR. TRILETZKY. Have a ruble.

(GREKOVA turns to flee, with a cry of pain, but is stopped by VOYNITZEV as he enters.)

VOYNITZEV. Fireworks!

GREKOVA. What?

VOYNITZEV. Don't run away! (*to PLATONOV*) We're staying! I don't know what you said, but you persuaded her! I *told* her you were the most eloquent man in the world! I won't forget this, Misha. Come on! I'm going to light the fireworks!

GREKOVA. (*to DR. TRILETZKY*) I'm going to watch the fireworks, I don't care about you. (*Exit VOYNITZEV, with GREKOVA after him. Enter ANNA PETROVNA.*)

DR. TRILETZKY. (*excited*) Fireworks! Fireworks! (*Exit DR. TRILETZKY.*)

PLATONOV. (*to ANNA PETROVNA*) My god! What have I done?

ANNA PETROVNA. Sasha's gone. She'll miss the fireworks.

PLATONOV. (*takes ANNA PETROVNA's hands in his*) What's going to become of us all?

ANNA PETROVNA. You seem just a tiny bit less married.

PLATONOV. How are we going to survive our lives?

ANNA PETROVNA. First of all by enjoying the fireworks.

(ANNA PETROVNA begins to lead PLATONOV off after the others. Enter GLAGOLYEV.)

GLAGOLYEV. Anna Petrovna! (*She turns back to him.*) Let me say at once that I should renounce the usual rights of a husband . . .

ANNA PETROVNA. And let me say one words to you, my friend.

GLAGOLYEV. Yes?

ANNA PETROVNA. Fireworks! (*Exit ANNA PE-TROVNA after PLATONOV. Enter PETRIN*)

PETRIN. What did she say? What did she say?

GLAGOLYEV. She said fireworks.

(*Exit GLAGOLYEV after ANNA PETROVNA, and PE-TRIN after GLAGOLYEV. Enter SOFYA.*)

SOFYA. (*to herself*) Is it ruin, or is it happiness? Is it the beginning of a new life, or is it the end of everything?

(*Enter COLONEL TRILETZKY.*)

COLONEL TRILETZKY. It's the fireworks! (*Exeunt COLONEL TRILETZKY and SOFYA after the others. Enter OSIP from under the trees.*)

VOYNITZEV. (*off*) Look out, everyone! We're starting! (*OSIP whips out a long-bladed hunting knife; and at the same moment there is the whoosh of a rocket taking off. OSIP stands gazing upwards, knife raised, as the co-loured stars burst in the sky. There is a collective sigh of satisfaction from the spectators, off. The stars fade. OSIP brings the knife down into the back of one of the garden chairs.*)

(*Curtain.*)

ACT TWO

Scene One

*A clearing in the forest. Right — the local schoolhouse. In
the background — the same tall trees as in the previous act. Here, though, they are bisected not by a
grassy garden walk, but by a railway line, which
comes straight down to the front of the stage, where it
passes between the wooden baulks of a rough level
crossing.*

*Before the curtain rises there is the sound of a goods train,
clanking and whistling as it passes through the auditorium. The curtain goes up to reveal the red tail light
of the train at the front of the stage, moving away
from us then disappearing among the smoke left by
the locomotive.*

*PLATONOV emerges from the smoke, stepping over the
rail on to the track, and walking dejectedly towards
us. When the smoke finally clears it reveals a brilliant moonlit night, as bright as day.*

PLATONOV. (*calls, gloomily*) Sasha . . . !
Sasha . . . !

(*A window in the schoolhouse opens, and SASHA looks
out, in her nightgown.*)

SASHA. Misha?
PLATONOV. Sasha . . .
SASHA. Sh! You'll wake the baby.
PLATONOV. Sasha . . .
SASHA. Are you drunk?
PLATONOV. Sasha, do you love me?

SASHA. Wait. I'll come out. (*The window closes. PLA-TONOV sinks gloomily down on to the step of the schoolhouse verandah. The door opens, and SASHA comes out.*) What's the time? Was that the goods or the passenger? Are the fireworks over?

PLATONOV. Do you, Sasha?

SASHA. You are a bit drunk. Aren't you, Misha?

PLATONOV. Do you love me?

SASHA. Misha! It took me hours to get him to sleep!

PLATONOV. Do you, though? I want to know.

SASHA. Of course I love you.

PLATONOV. Why?

SASHA. Why?

PLATONOV. Name one single good thing in me that you love me for! Name one good quality that could possibly make me love you!

SASHA. You're in a funny mood, aren't you, Misha? Obviously I love you! You're my husband!

PLATONOV. That's the only reason you love me, because I'm your husband?

SASHA. Misha, sometimes I don't understand you at all.

PLATONOV. Don't you? (*He laughs*) No, you're a fool, aren't you. A complete fool. You should have been a fly. In the land of the flies, with your brains, you'd have been the cleverest fly of all. (*He kisses her brow.*) Where should we be if you understood me, if you realised how little there was to love in me?

SASHA. What happened? Didn't you enjoy the fireworks?

PLATONOV. Fireworks, fireworks . . . I ran away, Sasha!

SASHA. From the fireworks?

PLATONOV. From myself ! Fled, in shame and terror!

Came running all the way back to you!

SASHA. (*laughs*) You're the fool, Misha!

PLATONOV. And I'm not drunk. I'm not drunk now. I certainly wasn't drunk then.

SASHA. When?

PLATONOV. When I told her she'd married a moral pygmy.

SASHA. Told who? Told Sofya Yegorovna?

PLATONOV. My tongue ran away with me! I behaved like a schoolboy! Postured, strutted, showed off . . .

SASHA. She's beautiful.

PLATONOV. Why did I say all those things? I didn't believe them! *She* believed them, though!

SASHA. I don't think I've ever seen anyone as beautiful as that.

PLATONOV. Anna Petrovna got a proposal of marriage.

SASHA. From Porfiry Semyonovich? What did she say?

PLATONOV. Nothing. He had a heart-attack.

SASHA. Oh no! Is he all right?

PLATONOV. Your brother bled him.

SASHA. They want may brother in the village. It's the storekeeper — he's very poorly. Had Kolya sobered up at all?

PLATONOV. I grandly mock people like Porfiry Semyonovich and Gerasim Kuzmich. But who's going to mock me? When are they going to start? It's ridiculous! I don't take bribes, I don't steal, I don't beat my wife, I think high-minded thoughts — and still I'm a scoundrel, a ridiculous scoundrel!

SASHA. Misha, you're talking nonsense. It's time you were in bed.

PLATONOV. Oh, my precious! My lovely silly little

noodle! I shouldn't think of you as a wife — I should put you in a glass case with a label on you. How did you and I ever manage to bring a baby into the world? You shouldn't be bearing children, my love; you should still be making little men out of dough. (*He tries to kiss her.*)

SASHA. (*refuses to be kissed*) Get away from me! Why did you marry me, if I was such a fool? I didn't force you to! You should have got yourself a clever one, if that's what you wanted! I'm going back to bed. (*Exit SASHA into the house.*)

PLATONOV. (*laughs*) Oh, and she can manage to lose her temper sometimes! But this is a great discovery! She's learning how to lose her little temper! (*He begins to follow her into the house.*) All hurt and cross, are we . . . ?

(*Enter ANNA PETROVNA from the shadows of the forest. She is wearing a riding habit and carrying a whip.*)

ANNA PETROVNA. Platonov! (*PLATONOV stops and turns*) I knew you wouldn't be asleep. How can anyone sleep on a night like this? God made the winter for sleeping! Come here, Platonov.

PLATONOV. (*reluctantly crosses to her*) What are you doing here?

ANNA PETROVNA. Taking a little walk in the moonlight. (*She leads him gently by the arm away from the house.*) What are *you* doing here? You disappeared without so much as a word of goodbye. You didn't think that I should let you get away with such discourtesy?

PLATONOV. I apologise.

ANNA PETROVNA. But what big eyes he has, out here in the moonlight! Don't be frightened — I'm not going to eat you.

PLATONOV. I see you are set upon some foolishness.

ANNA PETROVNA. Foolishness comes with age. Platonov.

PLATONOV. And age excuses it. But you're not old. You're as young as the summer itself. You have your life in front of you.

ANNA PETROVNA. I don't want my life in front of me — I want it now! Because, yes, I am young! It's terrible how young I am! I can feel it stirring in me like the night air among the trees.

PLATONOV. Anna Petrovna, I beg you to think what you're doing.

ANNA PETROVNA. I have thought.

PLATONOV. All your intelligence, all your beauty, all your youth — and you have to come to me! You come bent on conquest, on storming a stronghold. But no great conquest will you have. I know I took a high tone with you before. But I realise, when I look back on my behaviour tonight, that I had no right to such a tone.

ANNA PETROVNA. Self-abasement is a form of pride. But what are we to do, Misha? We've got to finish the thing one way of another.

PLATONOV. Finish it? We haven't started it!

ANNA PETROVNA. How can you say that? How can you lie to me, on such a night as this, beneath such a sky? Tell your lies in the autumn, if you must, in the gloom and the mud, but not now, not here. You're being watched! Look up, you absurd man! A thousand eyes, all shining with indignation! You must be good and true, just as all this is good and true. Don't break this silence with your little words! (*She takes his hands, and they sit down on the timbers of the crossing, facing each other.*) There's no man in the world I could ever love as I love you. There's no woman in the world you could ever love as you love me. Let's take that love; and all the rest, that so torments you — we'll leave that to others to worry about.

PLATONOV. (*kisses her hands*) Odysseus was worth the sirens' song, but I'm no Odysseus, you lovely siren of the forest. If only I could give you happiness! But I can't, and I shan't. I shall do what I've done to every woman who has thrown herself at me; I shall make you unhappy!

ANNA PETROVNA. Are you really such a terrible Don Juan? You look so handsome in the moonlight!

PLATONOV. I know myself! The only stories that end happily are the ones that don't have me in them.

ANNA PETROVNA. Such a solemn face! It's a woman who's come to call, not a wild animal! All right — if you really hate it all so much I'll go away again. Is that what you want? I'll go away, and everything will be just as it was before. Yes . . . ? (*She laughs.*) Idiot! Take it! Snatch it! Seize it! What more do you want? Smoke it to the end, like a cigarette — pinch it out — tread it under your heel. Be human! (*She gently shakes him.*) You funny creature! A woman who loves you — a woman you love — fine summer weather. What could be simpler than that? (*She lays here head on his knees.*) You don't realise how hard life is for me.

PLATONOV. I shan't make it easier.

ANNA PETROVNA. And yet life is what I long for. Everything is alive, nothing is ever still. We're surrounded by life. We must live, too, Misha! Leave all the problems for tomorrow. Tonight, on this night of nights, we'll simply live!

PLATONOV. Let me make one last appeal. As a man of honour . . .

ANNA PETROVNA. (*embraces him*) Don't be stupid, Misha. I'm never going to let you go. You're mine!

PLATONOV. One final plea . . .

ANNA PETROVNA. If I can't do it nicely I'll take you by force! (*She puts her whip round his neck.*) Come on!

PLATONOV. It'll end badly.

ANNA PETROVNA. You should write stern editorials in the newspapers.

PLATONOV. You'll see.

ANNA PETROVNA. You'd be good at that.

PLATONOV. Where are we going, then?

ANNA PETROVNA. To the old summerhouse!

SASHA. (*calls sleepily, off*) Misha! (*PLATONOV and ANNA PETROVNA stop.*)

PLATONOV. Sasha . . . I'd forgotten all about her.

ANNA PETROVNA. So had I.

PLATONOV. How could I just forget about her?

ANNA PETROVNA. It wouldn't be for the first time.

SASHA. (*off*) Misha?

PLATONOV. I'll just get her off to sleep.

ANNA PETROVNA. Platonov!

PLATONOV. I can't leave her wondering where I am!

SASHA. (*off*) Where are you, Misha?

ANNA PETROVNA. But that might take another hour!

PLATONOV. Two minutes! She falls asleep like a child if I stroke her head. Wait here!

ANNA PETROVNA. If you're not back in two minutes . . .

PLATONOV. I'll be back!

ANNA PETROVNA. . . . . . I'll come in and fetch you!

(*Enter SASHA from the house.*)

SASHA. Misha?

PLATONOV. Here, my love! (*Exeunt PLATONOV and SASHA into the house. Enter OSIP from beneath the trees.*)

ANNA PETROVNA. Who's that?

OSIP. See that stump there? Rotten. So it glows in the dark. As if a dead man had risen from his grave.

ANNA PETROVNA. Osip . . .

OSIP. My mother used to say that under every stump that glows in the dark there's a sinner buried. That's why the stump glows. To make us pray for his soul. I used to wonder how there could be so many glowing stumps in the forest.

ANNA PETROVNA. How long have you been there, Osip?

OSIP. Long enough.

ANNA PETROVNA. Were you spying?

OSIP. I thought you were some kind of saint.

ANNA PETROVNA. Used you to be in love with me then, Osip?

OSIP. If you'd have told me to walk into the fire, I'd have walked into the fire.

ANNA PETROVNA. You're not still in love with me?

OSIP. That's not in my place to say. (*He weeps.*)

ANNA PETROVNA. Oh, and he's crying. Come on, we'll be friends again. You can bring me some more baby owls. Just so long as you promise me one thing . . .

OSIP. If I'd had a gun in my hands as I stood there!

ANNA PETROVNA. One thing, Osip: you won't ever hurt him. Promise?

OSIP. I'll promise this: if he should ever hurt you . . . (*He pulls out his hunting-knife.*)

(*Enter PLATONOV from the house.*)

PLATONOV. She's asleep! (*OSIP disappears beneath the trees.*)

ANNA PETROVNA. Misha! We must go! Quickly! Before anything else happens!

(*She take his arm, and they start into the forest. Enter DR. TRILETZKY, drunker than before.*)

DR. TRILETZKY. Who's that? That Sasha? Sasha! (*PLATONOV returns. ANNA PETROVNA remains hidden among the trees.*)

PLATONOV. Sh! Sasha's asleep! You'll wake her!

DR. TRILETZKY. Oh, it's you. Thought it was Sasha.

PLATONOV. Sasha's asleep.

DR. TRILETZKY. Took Porfiry Semyonovich home, you see. Thought I'd just ask Sasha if I could sleep here.

PLATONOV. Well, you can't ask her, because she's asleep.

DR. TRILETZKY. She's asleep?

PLATONOV. Fast asleep.

DR. TRILETZKY. I'll wake her up.

PLATONOV. Don't wake her up!

DR. TRILETZKY. Can't find my way home, Misha.

PLATONOV. Well, you can't stay here.

DR. TRILETZKY. Sasha won't mind.

PLATONOV. Don't go in there!

DR. TRILETZKY. (*calls*) Sasha!

PLATONOV. Listen! Listen! The village storekeeper— he's ill. You've got to go. (*DR. TRILETZKY flaps his hand dismissively.*) It's urgent . . . You've got to operate!

DR. TRILETZKY. Operate?

PLATONOV. You know you like operating!

DR. TRILETZKY. Can't operate now, Misha! It's the middle of the night! It's past the passenger!

PLATONOV. That wasn't the passenger. That was only the goods.

DR. TRILETZKY. (*goes towards the house*) Can't operate now. Haven't got my little bag.

PLATONOV. (*turns him back towards the village*) Come on. You've got your penknife.

DR. TRILETZKY. (*heads back towards the house*) Have a little sleep first.

PLATONOV. (*turns him round*) Have a little sleep afterwards. (*DR. TRILETZKY begins to go off the way he came. ANNA PETROVNA emerges from the shadows, and PLATONOV goes to join her. DR. TRILETZKY turns back towards the house.*)

DR. TRILETZKY. Think my little bag may be in here.

PLATONOV. (*intercepts him*) Have you no shame? Have you no honour?

DR. TRILETZKY. Not at one o'clock in the morning, Misha!

PLATONOV. What sort of man are you, Nikolai? What god to you serve? What are you doing with your life? Do you think you were put in this world just to eat and drink and behave like a swine?

DR. TRILETZKY. I'm a swine, Misha, you're right.

PLATONOV. What are we all doing with our lives. (*He weeps.*) What god do *I* serve?

DR. TRILETZKY. You're crying! Don't cry, Misha!

PLATONOV. What's going to become of us all? Dirt in the ground! That's all we shall ever make!

DR. TRILETZKY. All right, Misha. I'll go and open him up.

(*Exit DR. TRILETZKY the way be entered. ANNA PETROVNA emerges from the shadows again.*)

ANNA PETROVNA. Has he gone?

PLATONOV. Yes, he's gone. Gone to save a human life. And what am *I* doing?

ANNA PETROVNA. (*puts an arm around his*

shoulders) *You're* going to save a human life. Your own life!

PLATONOV. It's not me who's coming with you. It's the devil at my back who says 'Go on, go on!' It's not me who obeys him — it's my weak flesh.

ANNA PETROVNA. (*moves away from him sharply*) Oh, for heaven's sake! (*She strikes him with her whip.*) If you want to come with me then come with me. If you don't then to hell with it! (*A shot off, followed by a wild cry of alarm.*) He's going to kill you! (*She throws her arms around him protectively.*)

PLATONOV. What? Who? Where?

ANNA PETROVNA. Osip! He's fetched a gun! He's going to kill you!

(*She drags PLATONOV into hiding under the trees. Enter VOYNITZEV and COLONEL TRILETZKY from the forest. They are both carrying sporting guns, and are both drunk.*)

VOYNITZEV. (*sees smoke curling from one of the barrels of his gun*) Was that me?

COLONEL TRILETZKY. My dear chap, another inch and it would have been *me* !

VOYNITZEV. My ears are still ringing!

COLONEL TRILETZKY. I said, you almost shot me!

VOYNITZEV. Great shock to me, too, but don't shout, you'll wake him up. (*He prods COLONEL TRILETZKY warningly with his gun.*)

COLONEL TRILETZKY. Yes, Sh! (*He puts the gun to his lips.*)

VOYNITZEV. Sh! (*He does the same. They cross to the house.*)

COLONEL TRILETZKY. Right outside his window!

VOYNITZEV. Biggest surprise of his life!

COLONEL TRILETZKY. Twenty-one gun salute!

(*They raise their guns to fire. Enter PLATONOV from the shadows.*)

PLATONOV. No! No!

VOYNITZEV. What the devil . . . ? (*They level their guns at PLATONOV.*)

COLONEL TRILETZKY. Halt! Who goes there!

VOYNITZEV. One more step and we'll shoot!

PLATONOV. It's me! It's me! Platonov! Misha!

VOYNITZEV. Misha?

PLATONOV. Don't shout!

COLONEL TRILETZKY. We're not shouting.

VOYNITZEV. We're shooting.

PLATONOV. Don't shout *or* shoot! You'll wake Sasha!

VOYNITZEV. Oh yes, Sasha.

COLONEL TRILETZKY. My little girl.

VOYNITZEV. Musn't wake Sasha.

PLATONOV. What are you doing here?

COLONEL TRILETZKY. (*to VOYNITZEV*) What are we doing here?

VOYNITZEV. (*to PLATONOV*) We're looking for you!

COLONEL TRILETZKY. Show you my new gun!

VOYNITZEV. Give you a surprise!

COLONEL TRILETZKY. Twenty-one gun salute!

VOYNITZEV. Twenty-one gun salute! (*They raise their guns to fire.*)

PLATONOV. *No!*

VOYNITZEV. Sh!

COLONEL TRILETZKY. Sh!

VOYNITZEV. Musn't wake Sasha.

PLATONOV. Right, now will you get out of here.

VOYNITZEV. We want you to come shooting with us!

PLATONOV. Shooting? It's the middle of the night! It's gone the goods—it's almost the passenger!

COLONEL TRILETZKY. His wife—charming girl . . .

VOYNITZEV. Sofya. You've met Sofya.

COLONEL TRILETZKY. She told me to take him out and shoot him. Take him out and shoot him?—Take him out shooting.

VOYNITZEV. Very difficult to see anything to shoot.

COLONEL TRILETZKY. You could shoot owls, she said.

VOYNITZEV. Very difficult to see owls.

COLONEL TRILETZKY. He's drunk, of course.

VOYNITZEV. First time in my life, Misha! Oh God, I'm so happy! (*He embraces PLATONOV.*)

PLATONOV. Keep that gun away from me, will you?

VOYNITZEV. Oh yes. Mustn't wake Sasha.

COLONEL TRILETZKY. Creep quietly away.

VOYNITZEV. Indians on the warpath. Not a sound. (*They begin to stumble away into the forest.*)

COLONEL TRILETZKY. I know what we can do!

VOYNITZEV. Sh! What?

COLONEL TRILETZKY. Serenade Anna Petrovna! Stand under her window and give her the old artillery serenade!

VOYNITZEV. How does that go?

COLONEL TRILETZKY. The twenty-one gun salute!

VOYNITZEV. Oh, the twenty-one gun salute! (*They raise their guns to fire.*)

PLATONOV. Go away!

VOYNITZEV. Oh yes. (*They guiltily place their guns against each other's lips.*)

COLONEL TRILETZKY. Sh!
VOYNITZEV. Sh!

(*Exeunt COLONEL TRILETZKY and VOYNITZEV into the forest. ANNA PETROVNA comes out of hiding.*)

ANNA PETROVNA. Misha!
PLATONOV. Coming, coming.
SASHA. (*off*) Misha?
PLATONOV. (*calls*) Coming!
ANNA PETROVNA. Misha, yes or no! (*Platonov hesitates.*)
PETRIN. (*off*) So where is she? (*ANNA PETROVNA looks around to see who this is.*) Who knows? Playing duets with Platonov! (*Exit PLATONOV into the house.*) Out in the woods with the colonel!
ANNA PETROVNA. (*to PLATONOV*) We might as well be in the centre of Petersburg!

(*She sees that PLATONOV has gone, and goes back into hiding. Enter PETRIN, supported by DR. TRILETZKY. PETRIN is in his shirtsleeves, and is even drunker than the doctor.*)

PETRIN. And where is our great lover of women? He's gone home with a heart attack! A moonlit night in June, and he lies down and has a heart attack!
DR. TRILETZKY. Now you follow the rails, look. Be home in no time. No one around . . . I think I'm just going to have a little sleep at my sister's here.
PETRIN. No one could accuse me of impatience, Kolya!
DR. TRILETZKY. Just step to one side when the train comes.

PETRIN. I own that woman! I own the clothes on her back! I own her stepson's underpants! All mine, Kolya! And what do I get in return? I get treated like dirt! Leant across by the servants! Spoken to like a pig! (*PETRIN starts away up the railway track.*) But thus far, Kolya! Thus far and no further! (*He stumbles over a sleeper and falls down on the track.*)

DR. TRILETZKY. (*calls, delighted*) Sasha! (*Enter PLATONOV from the house.*) Misha . . . !

PLATONOV. Well?

DR. TRILETZKY. It's Gerasim Kuzmich! He's been with the village girls again!

PLATONOV. And the storekeeper?

DR. TRILETZKY. The storekeeper?

PLATONOV. He's dying, Kolya!

DR. TRILETZKY. Yes, well, the storekeeper . . . (*Dr. TRILETZKY retreats from PLATONOV back in the direction he came from.*) I suppose it doesn't matter if *I* die . . .

(*Exit DR. TRILETZKY. Enter ANNA PETROVNA from under the trees.*)

ANNA PETROVNA. Platonov! Are you coming with me or not? Because I'm not going back behind that tree.

PLATONOV. All right. All right . . .

ANNA PETROVNA. If it's not your brother-in-law it's your father-in-law. If it's not your father-in-law it's . . .

(*Enter Sasha from the house.*)

SASHA. Misha! What's happening? What are you doing out here? Is that someone with you? (*She laughs.*) Anna Petrovna!

ANNA PETROVNA. Alexandra Ivanovna.

SASHA. What in the name of goodness are you doing here at this time of night? You're dressed for driving . . . And you're inviting us! Oh, what a lovely idea! It's such a beautiful night! Do let's go, Misha! I'll get dressed! (*Exit SASHA into the house.*)

ANNA PETROVNA. So now what are you going to do, Platonov?

PLATONOV. I don't know.

ANNA PETROVNA. Well, I shall be in the old summerhouse. If you want to see me you must come to me there.

PLATONOV. But what shall I tell Sasha?

ANNA PETROVNA. That's your business! I'm not going to lie to your wife for you! (*Exit ANNA PETROVNA*)

PLATONOV. Anna Petrovna . . . ! (*He turns and goes towards the house.*) Sasha . . . !

(*Enter Dr. TRILETZKY.*)

DR. TRILETZKY. And another thing.

PLATONOV. You still haven't gone?

DR. TRILETZKY. I'm going! One word of advice first, my friend! If you're going to preach at people then you must preach what you practise!

PLATONOV. Come here! (*He advances on him.*)

DR. TRILETZKY. (*backs away*) I'm going, I'm going!

PLATONOV. No, you're not. You're not in a fit condition to see a patient. Sasha will have to put you to bed.

DR. TRILETZKY. Bed! Go to bed?

(*Enter SASHA, dressed, from the house.*)

SASHA. I've always longed to go for a drive in the moonlight! Where are we going?

PLATONOV. We're not going anywhere. You've got to put your brother to bed.

SASHA. Kolya! Oh, no!

PLATONOV. He can sleep in the classroom.

DR. TRILETZKY. (*bewildered*) Sleep? Lie down?

PLATONOV. Quickly, now! I think he's going to be sick!

SASHA. (*leads DR. TRILETZKY into the house*) And you'll wake the baby, so then I'll have to get *him* back to sleep.

DR. TRILETZKY. Everything's going round. It's all turned back to front!

PLATONOV. I'll tell Anna Petrovna we'll come another time, shall I?

SASHA. Another time, yes, another time. (*Exeunt SASHA and DR. TRILETZKY into the house.*)

PLATONOV. (*to himself*) I'm going, then. (*He begins to move irresolutely off.*) It's not as if I were the only man in the world to behave like this . . . (*He falls over PETRIN.*)

PETRIN. They all walk over me.

PLATONOV. Gerasim Kuzmich . . .

PETRIN. Not going to go on walking over me.

PLATONOV. You've been with the village girls again. (*He sits down on the rail beside PETRIN.*) We're all the same. One word from a woman, and that's all we can think of.

PETRIN. One word from me, and up the sign will go! 'To be sold at public auction.' (*Enter SOFYA from the forest, very nervous, her face concealed. She tries to see into the windows of the house.*)

PLATONOV. Is that what our lives are going to amount to? One long procession of women?

SOFYA. (*taps at the window and whispers desperately*) Misha!

PLATONOV. Sasha! My little noodle! That settles it! I must have been mad! (*He burries across to SOFYA.*) Here I am, my treasure! I'll never leave you! Not for a moment! not ever!

SOFYA. Misha! Oh, Misha!

PLATONOV. Sofya!

SOFYA. (*throws herself into his arms*) I waited for you after the fireworks! Waited and waited! I was sure you'd come! I made my husband go out shooting with the colonel — they're both drunk — they'll shoot each other — I must be mad! You said you would, Misha! You promised you would!

PLATONOV. Would what?

SOFYA. Uproot us both!

PLATONOV. Oh yes.

SOFYA. Uproot me, Misha!

PLATONOV. Yes, but not here! (*Sasha opens the window of the house.*)

SASHA. Misha!

PLATONOV. (*to SOFYA, warningly*) Sasha!

SASHA. Was that you tapping on the window?

PLATONOV. (*to SASHA*) No? (*to SOFYA*) In the old summerhouse! (*to SASHA*) Yes! Only me! (*to SOFYA*) No!

SASHA. No?

PLATONOV. (*to SASHA*) Yes! (*to SOFYA*) Not in the old summerhouse!

SASHA. What?

PLATONOV. (*to SASHA*) Nothing! (*to SOFYA*) In the new summerhouse! (*Exit SOFYA into the forest.*)

SASHA. I can's understand a word. (*SASHA closes the*

window. PLATONOV pulls PETRIN up into a sitting positions.)

PLATONOV. Gerasya! Help me! What am I going to do? Which way, Gerasya? Which one — old or new? (*There is the sound of distant train whistle, and a tiny star of light appears on the horizon at the end of the railway track.*) Train . . . ! YES! I'll run to the station! Go away, and never come back . . . !

PETRIN. Never get her married to him now.

PLATONOV. But she is, isn't she? She's in love with me, too!

PETRIN. I'll take her to court.

PLATONOV. So this is happiness, then. This is what it feels like . . . But which one of them, Gerasya? Which one of them?

(*Enter SASHA from the house.*)

SASHA. Misha! Where are you! What's all this about a summerhouse? (*PLATONOV drops PETRIN back on to the track, and flees in the direction taken by ANNA PETROVNA. But he meets OSIP emerging from beneath the trees, and diverts to go off in the direction taken by SOFYA.*) Osip! What's happening? I don't understand . . . Osip, what are you doing? (*OSIP lies down across the level crossing. The headlight of the approaching train grows slowly bigger.*) You can't lie there! Osip, get up! The train's coming!

OSIP. (*sobs*) He's gone to her! Gone to Anna Petrovna! And she loves him! She loves him!

SASHA. You're lying.

OSIP. God strike me down — I heard every word!

SASHA. He's left me, then! He's left me! Kill me, Lord! Mother of God, kill me! (*The whistle of the approaching*

*train. SASHA runs towards it with outstretched arms.
OSIP jumps up and runs after her.)*

OSIP. No! No! (*They stumble over PETRIN, who sits
up. They stop and turn round to gaze at him in
astonishment.*)

PETRIN. Yes! Yes! You'll see! Tomorrow! (*SASHA
and OSIP drag PETRIN clear of the track as the headlight widens, and the roar of the approaching train and
the scream of the whistle rise to a crescendo. The locomotive emerges from the darkness and comes towards us just
as the curtain falls. The roar of the train and the scream of
the whistle continue through the auditorium in the darkness, until the lights come up for:-)*

SCENE TWO

*The combined schoolroom and living-room inside the
PLATONOV's house. The wooden baulks of the
level crossing now form the rough timber floor of the
room. In the rear wall of the room are a window and a
door; beyond it are the same tall trees of the forest as
in the earlier scenes. There is a sofa in the room, a
cupboard, a table with two chairs, and all the signs of
a cramped, muddied and sleazy life. It is early
evening.*

*PLATONOV is lying on the sofa, fast asleep, with a straw
hat covering his face. Enter SOFYA.*

SOFYA. Platonov! Wake up! (*She shakes him.*) Misha!
(*She takes the hat off his face.*) How could you put this
filthy object on your face! Ugh! What a mess you are!
Haven't washed, have you? And look at this pig-sty! It's
only three weeks since your wife walked out. It would

break her heart if she could see it now . . . Misha, I'm talking to you! Get up!

PLATONOV. Um?

SOFYA. Wake up, will you!

PLATONOV. Just a minute.

SOFYA. Now!

PLATONOV. (*sits up*) Oh, it's you.

SOFYA. Yes, it's me! (*She holds her watch in front of his eyes.*) Look!

PLATONOV. Right. (*He lies down again.*)

SOFYA. Platonov!

PLATONOV. What do you want? (*He sits up.*) What is it?

SOFYA. Look at the time!

PLATONOV. Fussing away again, are you, Sofya?

SOFYA. Yes, I'm fussing away again! Look at this watch, will you! Now tell me what it says.

PLATONOV. Half-past six.

SOFYA. Half-past six, yes.

PLATONOV. Not time to get up yet.

SOFYA. Half-past six in the *evening*. Have you forgotten what we agreed?

PLATONOV. What did we agree? Don't talk in riddles, please. I'm not up to it today.

SOFYA. You have forgotten. What's the matter with you? Your eyes are red. You look as if you've been crumpled up into a ball and thrown away . . . You're not ill, are you . . . ? What we agreed was to meet in the usual place. At six o'clock.

PLATONOV. Go on.

SOFYA. What do you mean, Go on? Aren't you ashamed of yourself? You gave me your word of honour! (*She sits beside him.*)

PLATONOV. I'd have kept it, too, if I hadn't fallen

asleep. You could see for yourself—I was fast asleep! I don't know what you're going on about.

SOFYA. Have you been on time for a single one of our meetings? Every day you give me your word of honour —and every day you break it! Why do you stop being yourself whenever I'm with you.

PLATONOV. (*jumps up, and walks up and down the room*) So, here you are.

SOFYA. Are you drunk?

PLATONOV. None of your business.

SOFYA. And that's very charming, I must say! (*She weeps.*)

PLATONOV. Women!

SOFYA. And don't start saying 'Women'! I'm not some poor simple village girl, and I'm not going to let myself be humiliated like this (*She weeps.*) My God! My God!

PLATONOV. Now that's enough.

SOFYA. It's barely three weeks since . . . Since that night! And already I'm only a shadow of myself! Where's the happiness you promised me? And where's all this going to end? Think, if you're so clever! Start thinking now, before it's too late! Sit down right here on this chair, clear everything else out of your head, and just think about this one single thing: what are you doing to me?

PLATONOV. I can't think. I've forgotten how to think. You think yourself! All your unhappiness comes from this irregular liaison!

SOFYA. I give myself to him, and he has the nerve to talk about an 'irregular liaison'!

PLATONOV. Oh, come on! We can't start quibbling over every word! I've ruined you; and that's all there is to say about it! And you're not the only one! Wait until your husband finds out!

SOFYA. You're afraid he's going to kill you?

PLATONOV. No. I'm afraid it's going to kill him.

SOFYA. He already knows!

PLATONOV. What?

SOFYA. Yes! I told him this afternoon.

PLATONOV. You're not serious!

SOFYA. Look at you. You're as white as a sheet. I don't know why I should love you. I must be mad!

PLATONOV. How did he take it?

SOFYA. Just like you. He was afraid. His skin went grey. He started to cry. Then he crumpled up. He went down and crawled on all fours . . . And he had just the same repellent look on his face as you have now.

PLATONOV. You've killed him! Do you realise that? How could you sit there and tell me it all so calmly? You've killed him! Did you . . . did you say it was me?

SOFYA. Of course. What else could I have said?

PLATONOV. You know what you've done, don't you? You've parted forever

SOFYA. Forever, yes. What alternative did I have?

PLATONOV. (*flaps his hand*) Well, you do whatever you think best. You're a better person than I am. You've got a cleverer head on your shoulders. You take the whole mess over! Just tell me what to do! Get me up on my feet again, if you have the power. And do it now, for the love of God, before I go out of my mind!

SOFYA. We'll leave tonight.

PLATONOV. The sooner the better.

SOFYA. I wrote to my mother about you. We'll go to her.

PLATONOV. Anywhere you like! Just as long as we get away from here!

SOFYA. Misha! This will be our new life, though! Do you see? Trust me, love! I'll get you up on your feet again! I'll make you work! We'll be proper people, Misha! We'll eat our bread in the sweat of our faces. We'll harden our hands. (*She lays her head on his chest.*) I'll work, too.

PLATONOV. What do you know about work?

SOFYA. Trust me, Misha, that's all you have to do! You raised me from the dead, and all my life will be a thank-offering for that. We'll leave tonight, then, on the evening train. Yes? I'll go and get ready at once. You get your things together. We'll meet at the usual place an hour from now. Let's say quarter to eight. Yes? You will be there?

PLATONOV. I shall be there.

SOFYA. Word of honour?

PLATONOV. I said—I shall be there!

SOFYA. Give me your word of honour.

PLATONOV. Word of honour.

SOFYA. I don't want to have to come looking for you again . . . Cheer up, then! (*She kisses him.*) We're going to start our lives afresh, Misha! By tomorrow you'll be a different man. We'll be breathing new air! We'll have new blood flowing in our veins!

PLATONOV. Of course we will . . . Did you say quarter past eight or quarter past nine?

SOFYA. Quarter to eight! Or we'll miss the train! I've got some money—we'll eat on the way. (*She laughs.*) And smarten yourself up a bit for the journey! (*SOFYA runs out of the house.*)

PLATONOV. (*to himself*) A new life! That's an old song! I've heard that one a few times! (*pause*) I'd better write to him. And to Sasha. They can have a little weep, and then they can forgive and forget. So it's goodbye to everyone, because tomorrow I'm going to be a different man! (*He opens the cupboard.*) What am I going to put my clean underwear in? I haven't got a suit-case . . . (*He takes one of the many bottles in the cup-*

board and pours himself a drink.) Goodbye, old school of mine! Goodbye, boys and girls! (*He drinks.*) Your kindly old teacher, the swine, is doing a bolt . . . Was that me drinking? What am I drinking for? I'm giving up drinking! Well, this is the last drink I shall ever have . . . So, sit down and write to Sasha . . . (*He lies down on the sofa.*) Sofya really does believe it all, doesn't she . . . Well, blessed are they that have faith . . . As long as she hasn't told Anna Petrovna . . . Letter from Anna Petrovna somewhere . . . Ought to open it, see what she wants . . . (*finds a number of unopened envelopes*) *Three* letters from her . . . Haven't opened any of them. (*finds more*) Hundreds of letters from her! She hasn't stopped writing, ever since that wild and crazy night . . . (*He opens the letter absently.*) Just so long as I don't have to come face to face with her! She'd get the truth out of me in . . . (*He reads.*) 'If you don't answer this one, either, I shall come round there and . . . '

(*A knock at the door. PLATONOV jumps up in alarm, then stands undecided. Another knock. PLATONOV conceals himself behind it as the door opens. Enter, cautiously, MARKO, with his satchel.*)

MARKO. Anyone at home?
PLATONOV. Who's this?
MARKO. Me, sir. That you, sir?
PLATONOV. (*cautiously*) Yes?
MARKO. Platonov?
PLATONOV. What of it?
MARKO. Mikhail Vasilyevich Platonov?
PLATONOV. What do you want?
MARKO. From the magistrate, sir! (*He hands an envelope round the door to PLATONOV.*)

PLATONOV. (*emerges from hiding, relieved*) From the magistrate? Oh . . . not *another* christening! (*He opens the envelope.*) Breeds like a rabbit, that man! (*He reads.*) 'You are hereby summoned . . . ' (*to MARKO*) Do you know what you look like, cowering away behind the door there?

MARKO. Yes, sir.

PLATONOV. Oh, you know, do you?

MARKO. Yes, sir.

PLATONOV. (*reads*) 'You are hereby summoned to appear before His Imperial Majesty's Justice of the Peace . . . ' (*to MARKO*) What do you look like, then?

MARKO. Like God sir.

PLATONOV. Like God?

MARKO. Made in the image and likeness, sir.

PLATONOV. Oh, yes. (*He reads.*) ' . . . before His Imperial Majesty's Justice of the Peace to answer a charge of indecent assault . . 'It's not an invitation!

MARKO. No, sir.

PLATONOV. It's a summons!

MARKO. Yes, sir.

PLATONOV. (*reads*) ' . . . a charge of indecent assault, which charge has been laid upon the complaint of Marya Yefimovna Grekova . . . '! (*He laughs.*) Well, dash me! Good old Beetle-juice! I didn't know she'd got it in her!

MARKO. Sign for it, then, will you, sir? Just here, sir.

PLATONOV. (*signs*) When's the case being heard . . . ? The day after tomorrow. I'll be there! She should have done this last summer!

MARKO. Thank you, sir. (*He holds out his hand.*) Drink your health, sir.

PLATONOV. You can drink it in tea. (*He takes the tea-caddy out of the cupboard.*) Where do you want it?

(*MARKO holds his pocket open. PLATONOV pours the tea straight in.*) What a little champion she is, though! Never expected that! Who have they got as witnesses?

MARKO. (*sorts through the subpoenas in his bag*) 'Dr. Nikolai Ivanovich Triletzky.'

PLATONOV. The doctor? He'll be a comic turn! Who else?

MARKO. 'Sofya Yegorovna Voynitzeva.'

PLATONOV. Sofya Yegorovna? She won't be there! She's going away . . . Oh . . . Oh, yes . . . Take Marya Yefimovna a message will you?

MARKO. Marya Yefimovna — message. Yes?

PLATONOV. Tell her I'm very sorry . . .

MARKO. Very sorry.

PLATONOV. But I can't accept her kind summons because I'm going away.

MARKO. Going away.

PLATONOV. Forever, tell her.

MARKO. Going away forever. Right.

PLATONOV. Say I behaved like a swine, but then I've behaved like a swine with everybody. Say I should have been happy to kiss her again, with proper respect, before the whole world in open court.

MARKO. Like a swine. In open court.

PLATONOV. All right. Do you know where she lives?

MARKO. Good seven miles from here, sir. (*He holds out his hand.*) Can't walk seven miles on a glass of tea, sir!

PLATONOV. All right — a ruble. A ruble there, a ruble back, and a ruble for remembering it. Three rubles when you get back here and tell me you've delivered it! Off you go, then. Oh, and Marko . . .

MARKO. Yes, sir?

PLATONOV. That's what God looks like, is it?

MARKO. So I humbly believe, sir. (*Exit MARKO.*)

PLATONOV. (*to himself*) First time in my life I've ever been brought to book by a woman! Usually you treat them like dirt, and what do they do?—They hang around your neck . . . Oh, yes—Sasha. I was writing to Sasha . . . (*He finds the heap of unopened letters.*) No, I wasn't. I was hiding these before Anna Petrovna . . . (*A sharp knock at the door. He gazes at the door, transfixed, then tries to stuff the letters away inside the cupboard. The door is flung open, and OSIP enters. The letters come sliding out of the cupboard again. (Over his shoulder.)* Anna Petrovna! This is a surprise. (*He turns and sees OSIP.*) Oh, it's you. What do you want? (*OSIP sits down.*) What's the matter with you? You look as if you'd been through all the ten plagues of Egypt. I feel as if I'd been through nine of them. You're nothing but skin and bone, though. Are you ill? What are you doing here?

OSIP. Saying goodbye.

PLATONOV. Why? Are you going away?

OSIP. Not me. You.

PLATONOV. Good God, so I am! But how do you know that?

OSIP. I just do.

PLATONOV. Clairvoyant, are you, Osip, on top of all your other skills?

OSIP. I know something else, too. I know where you're going.

PLATONOV. Do you indeed! That's more than I know! Well, this is something that interests me. Where *am* I going?

OSIP. You're going to hell.

PLATONOV. I see. Quite a journey. You're not planning to be the driver of the train that takes me there, by any chance?

OSIP. (*takes out his hunting knife*) I used to have a lot of respect for you. Thought you were the great man . . . I've watched you these past weeks, though, you see. Slipping off into the forest at all hours of the day and night . . . Well, that's no business of mine, who the general's widow meets on her rides through the forest. But I saw something else tonight. I saw the young mistress come running down here. And I waited. And I saw her go running back again. So then I went and fetched my knife. Because I reckon you're making a fool of the general's widow, and I'm not having that. (*He stands up and seizes PLATONOV's arm.*)

PLATONOV. No! No! I've got a family! I've go a wife and child to support! (*OSIP raises the knife.*)

(*Enter SASHA through the front door*

SASHA. (*screams*) Misha! No! No! (*She tries to protect PLATONOV.*) Don't hurt him! Don't touch him!

OSIP. (*backs away*) Oh, it's you. You're still around, are you. Can't kill him in front of you . . . Anyway, you're back . . . I *will* kill him, though! He won't ever get away from me! (*Exit OSIP.*)

SASHA. Are you all right?

PLATONOV. Oh, my arm! He twisted my arm! (*He sits down on the sofa.*)

SASHA. Lie down. Put the cushion under your head. (*She settles the cushion for him.*)

PLATONOV. Don't fuss, my pet. I'm perfectly all right.

SASHA. Where does it hurt?

PLATONOV. I'm all right! Don't worry . . . He was going to kill me! He was! He was going to kill me! You were only just in time, Sasha! Another minute and you'd have been a widow! (*He kisses her hand.*) Oh, Sasha! Oh, my treasure . . . ! Are you at your father's? How is he?

SASHA. He's all right . . . Misha, it's little Vova. That's why I came. He's ill, poor mite. He's running a terrible fever. The last two nights he's just cried all night. (*She weeps.*) Oh, Misha, I'm so worried! What am I going to do? If he died, Misha . . . What would become of us then?

PLATONOV. Yes . . . But God won't take our little boy away from you, Sasha. Why should he punish you? Look after him, Sasha, and I swear to you I'll make a man of him. I haven't been much of a man myself, I know, but as a father I shall be mighty! Oh, my arm! He hasn't broken something, has he . . . ? Don't cry, love! (*He pulls her head down on to his chest.*) You're home again. Why did you ever leave? I love you, lass! I love you deeply! My sins are black, I know, but what can we do? You'll just have to forgive me, won't you?

SASHA. Is the affair over, then?

PLATONOV. The affair . . . What a word to choose!

SASHA. Or isn't it over?

PLATONOV. What can I say? There never was an affair. It's just some kind of absurd nonsense. You should never have let yourself be upset by it. And if it's not over yet then it soon will be!

SASHA. When?

PLATONOV. Sooner rather than later, I should imagine. Sofya isn't the one for me. The ferment hasn't quite died down in her yet,but, believe me, Sofya won't be your rival for long . . . Sasha, what's the matter?

SASHA. Sofya? It's *Sofya* that you're having an affair with?

PLATONOV. You didn't know?

SASHA. Sofya? But that's terrible!

PLATONOV. Sasha, don't torment me any more! I'm in agony with my arm as it is! Why did you leave me, then? You mean, it wasn't because of Sofya?

SASHA. I thought it was Anna Petrovna! That was bad enough! But another man's wife! That's vile, Misha, that's wicked! I should never have thought it of you! Well, God give you happiness, the pair of you! (*She goes to the door.*)

PLATONOV. Don't talk like that, Sasha! I don't want happiness! Don't go, Sasha! (*He goes after her.*) Don't leave me! Could you truly never forgive me?

SASHA. Could you ever forgive yourself?

PLATONOV. That's an interesting question. (*He kisses her head.*) You don't have to go. I am truly penitent. And if you're not here it's going to be a dismal progression of vodka and squalor and men trying to murder me. If you won't stay as a wife, then stay as a nurse! All right, I've stolen my friend's wife — I'm Sofya's lover — and for all I know I may yet be Anna Petrovna's, too. You've every right to be indignant! But who will ever love you as I love you? Who will you cook dinner for? Who will you over-salt the soup for? (*He picks her up.*) Who's going to pick you up and carry you? How will you ever live without me?

SASHA. Put me down! My life is destroyed, and all you can do is joke about it! (*She gets away from him.*) You must know it's not a joke! How an I live without you? — How could I possibly live *with* you? (*She sobs.*)

PLATONOV. Off you go, then. And God go with you. (*He kisses her on the head, then lies down on the sofa again.*) I do understand.

SASHA. You've broken up our family. We were so happy and peaceful! There was no one on earth as happy as I was. What have you done, Misha? You'll never turn

back now . . . Don't come and visit us. Father will
bring Vova to see you . . . (*She looks at him for a moment, then round the room, then goes out.*)

PLATONOV. (*to himself*) Well, there's someone who's
starting a new life . . . Oh, but my God, the pain of it,
the pain . . . Poor little Sasha! She's a saint! She's got
every right to throw the first stone . . . What was I
doing? (*He takes a drink.*) I was going to write to
Sasha . . . No, I was going to . . . keep Anna Petrovna out! (*He hurries to the front door and bolts it.*)

(*ANNA PETROVNA appears at the window.*)

ANNA PETROVNA. Are you alone? (*PLATONOV
spins guiltily round.*) What are you doing? Don't you
recognise me? Have you forgotten who I am?

PLATONOV. Anna Petrovna . . . (*He crosses to the
window, But ANNA PETROVNA has disappeared. To
himself:*) Quick! Before she comes back! (*He hurries to
the front door, unbolts it, and opens it to escape. In walks
ANNA PETROVNA. PLATONOV retreats in front of
her.*)

ANNA PETROVNA. (*reproachfully*) Platonov!

PLATONOV. Anna Petrovna . . .

ANNA PETROVNA. Come here, Platonov. Why are
you running away from me? (*PLATONOV attempts to
stuff the letters into the cupboard behind his back.*) Never
mind that. It's too late now to start tidying up. Come
here! (*PLATONOV goes over to her. She gives him her
hand.*) Why won't you look at me, Platonov?

PLATONOV. I'm ashamed of myself. (*He kisses her
hand.*)

ANNA PETROVNA. What are you ashamed about?

PLATONOV. Everything.

ANNA PETROVNA. I see. You've seduced some poor girl, have you?

PLATONOV. Something like that.

ANNA PETROVNA. What are we going to do with you, Platonov? Who is it?

PLATONOV. You don't know?

ANNA PETROVNA. I'm asking you.

PLATONOV. I can't tell you.

ANNA PETROVNA. Perhaps we should sit down. (*They sit down on the sofa.*) Well, we shall find out, who it is, young man, we shall find out. Why do you have to put on this hangdog performance in front of me, though? I know your black heart of old.

PLATONOV. Don't ask me, Anna Petrovna! Talk, by all means, but no questions. I'm not up to being cross-examined today.

ANNA PETROVNA. Very well. Didn't you get my letters?

PLATONOV. Yes.

ANNA PETROVNA. So why didn't you come and see us?

PLATONOV. I couldn't.

ANNA PETROVNA. Why ever not?

PLATONOV. You're asking questions . . . ! I just couldn't.

ANNA PETROVNA. You knew we needed you. Sergey and Sofya are behaving very badly. Terrible sulks and silences. You wouldn't think they were still on their honeymoon. And all because we didn't have our clever fool there to entertain us . . . Or didn't you read my letters?

PLATONOV. Of course I read them.

ANNA PETROVNA. Sit up straight . . . Anyone would think you were ashamed of what happened that night.

PLATONOV. I've been ill.

ANNA PETROVNA. You're lying.

PLATONOV. I'm lying. There's no point in asking me anything.

ANNA PETROVNA. What sort of mess is this? You're drinking, are you?

PLATONOV. (*spreads his hands helplessly*) It's the holidays.

ANNA PETROVNA. It's the same story as last summer, isn't it.

PLATONOV. I'll stop, I'll stop.

ANNA PETROVNA. Word of honour?

PLATONOV. Word of honour.

ANNA PETROVNA. On second thoughts I won't put you to the trouble of keeping your word. Where's the drink? (*PLATONOV indicates the cupboard.*) You ought to be ashamed of yourself! Have you no character at all? Look at the mess in this cupboard! (*She finds the letters.*) I see. No wonder they had so little effect on you . . . Look at it all, though! Your wife's going to have something to say when she comes back! You do want her back, don't you?

PLATONOV. All I want is for you to stop asking me questions! And to stop trying to make me look you in the eye!

ANNA PETROVNA. Which bottle is the drink in?

PLATONOV. All of them.

ANNA PETROVNA. All of them? It's like a distillery in here! We'll have to get your wife back. You'll just have to make it up with her as best you can . . . It was no part of my plans to get you divorced. I don't mind sharing you . . . Now, I'm going to empty all this foul stuff out of the window. Some vile backyard brew, is it . . . ? (*She pours a little into a glass and tastes it.*) No, it isn't —

it's good vodka! All right, then, we'll drink a glass of it first, shall we? Yes? Just a drop to wish it goodbye. And a drop for me . . . To the wicked of this world! Of whom you're one . . . ! Not at all bad, this vodka. You have a little discrimination, at any rate . . . All right. (*She hands him bottles to carry.*) Out it goes . . . Pity to waste it all, though . . . One more drink first, yes?

PLATONOV. If you like.

ANNA PETROVNA. (*pours*) The quicker we drink it the sooner it will be gone.

PLATONOV. (*raises his glass*) Sobriety!

ANNA PETROVNA. Sobriety! (*They drink.*) Why don't we sit down? Put the bottles on the floor for the moment . . . Did you miss me?

PLATONOV. Every minute of every day.

ANNA PETROVNA. Then why didn't you come and see me?

PLATONOV. I'm dying, my dear, I'm dying! Dying of guilt and melancholy! I'm a soul in torment! Then you arrive, and what happens?—I feel a little better.

ANNA PETROVNA. Why can't you be like other people, you silly man? Why do you always have to be some kind of fallen archangel?

PLATONOV. My dear, what can I do?

ANNA PETROVNA. What can you do? You can stop drinking. You can stop lying here all day. You can wash a little more often. And you can come and see me. (*She gets to her feet.*) Come on! Let's go up to my house now!

PLATONOV. Go to your house? No, no!

ANNA PETROVNA. Yes, come on! Come and talk to Sergey and Sofya! Come and pick a few quarrels!

PLATONOV. No, no, no!

ANNA PETROVNA. Why on earth not?

PLATONOV. I can't.

ANNA PETROVNA. Of course you can! Come on — put your hat on!

PLATONOV. I'm not setting foot outside this house!

ANNA PETROVNA. (*puts his hat on his head*) Don't be idiotic! (*She takes him by the arm.*) Now, then. Left, right . . . ! Come on, Platonov! Quick march . . . ! Oh, really, Misha!

PLATONOV. I'm not going. I want to stay at home, and that's that!

ANNA PETROVNA. I see. Listen, Platonov . . . Sit down . . . (*They both sit.*) Do you know what's happening today? Porfiry Semyonovich is taking the train into town, and tomorrow he's going to buy the estate. He's going to settle all our debts. So I shall have money, Platonov, and I'm going to lend you some, and you're going to go away somewhere fro a month or two.

PLATONOV. Go away? Where to?

ANNA PETROVNA. Moscow . . . Petersburg . . . Wherever you like! All right? Do go, Misha. You absolutely must get away from here. Get out and about, see people, go to the theatre, have a complete change. And once the estate is sold *I* shan't have to be here. If you like, love, I'll come with you. Would you like that? We'll take drives together, we'll go for long walks. By the time we get back we shall be quite different people!

PLATONOV. It's a delightful idea. But, alas, impossible. I *am* going away, Anna Petrovna. I'm going tonight. But not with you.

ANNA PETROVNA. Well, please yourself . . . Where are you going?

PLATONOV. Away. (*pause*) Forever.

ANNA PETROVNA. Oh, nonsense! (*She drinks.*) Rubbish!

PLATONOV. It's not nonsense, my dear. I am going!

And it will be forever!

ANNA PETROVNA. But whatever for? You funny man.

PLATONOV. Don't ask me! But this is the last time we shall see each other. Forget the blackguard that was Platonov. He's going to disappear off the face of the earth! Perhaps we shall meet again many years from now, when we're both old — old enough to laugh together and shed an ancient tear or two over the past. As the present will mercifully have become. But in the meantime — forget him. (*He kisses her hand.*)

ANNA PETROVNA. But what's happened to you?

PLATONOV. You'll find out soon enough. But in your horror when you do, try not to curse me. I shall have been punished already by my separation from you.

ANNA PETROVNA. (*through her tears*) I can't think you've done anything so very terrible . . . And you'll never survive without me . . . I'm a little tiny bit drunk . . . We could all live so happily!

PLATONOV. Just leave me, my dear. Just say goodbye and leave me.

ANNA PETROVNA. One more for old times' sake?

PLATONOV. All right.

ANNA PETROVNA. If we're going to drink let's drink. (*She pours.*) You die if you drink. But then you die if you don't drink. (*She drinks.*) I'm one, too, Platonov. I'm a drinker . . . Another glass? No, I mustn't, or the words will go. Then what shall I have left? Oh, Misha, it's terrible to be an educated woman. An educated woman with nothing to do. What am I here for? Why am I alive? (*She laughs.*) They should make me a professor somewhere, or a director of something . . . If I were a diplomat I'd turn the whole world upside down . . . An educated woman . . . And nothing to do.

PLATONOV. We're both in sorry case.

ANNA PETROVNA. Won't you stay? You do . . . love me, don't you? You funny man. Don't you?

PLATONOV. How could any mortal man not love you?

ANNA PETROVNA. You love me—I love you; what more do you want . . . ? Why didn't you come to me that night . . . ? That wild night . . . Such a strange month it's been. Their honeymoon month. A sort of honeymoon for all of us. A month of wild honey.

PLATONOV. Please go now. If you stay I shall tell you everything, and if I tell you I shall kill myself. (*He takes her to the door.*) Goodbye. Be happy. (*He embraces and kisses her.*) We shall never see each other again.

ANNA PETROVNA. That depends upon whether I can catch him at the station.

PLATONOV. Catch him? Catch whom?

ANNA PETROVNA. Porfiry Semyonovich. He's getting the evening train. He'll have all the money for buying the estate. He can easily give me some of it. That's all we need, my love! (*Exit ANNA PETROVNA.*)

PLATONOV. (*to himself*) If only we could have gone away together! What would it have been? A few weeks. No more. What's that out of a whole lifetime? I could have seen Moscow again . . . I suppose I could ask Sofya to postpone our departure . . . We're going to spend the rest of our lives together—she could scarcely object to waiting for a week or two.

(*PLATONOV opens the front door to run after ANNA PETROVNA. There on the doorstep stands VOY-NITZEV. PLATONOV falls back, abashed, and retires to the far side of the room.*)

VOYNITZEV. One gift and one gift only did God bestow upon me in this life. One precious gift. And then he took it away from me again. (*PLATONOV sits down at the table, and hides his head in his hands.*) What am I? I'm nothing. I'm not very clever. I'm no great figure of a man . . . Whereas you have everything. Intelligence, looks, spirit. But they weren't enough for you. You had to have the one thing I possessed — my happiness (*He breaks down.*) Give her back to me, Platonov! You've so much fortune in your life! So much happiness! Give her back to me!

PLATONOV. If I had a gun I'd shoot myself.

VOYNITZEV. (*laughs through his tears*) That's what I cam here for! To challenge you! Or even . . . God forgive me, I don't know what I was going to do! (*He takes a revolver out of his pocket and tosses it down on the table between them.*) And what happens? I break down and cry . . . I'm sorry, Misha! Hopeless, hopeless! I'm sorry! (*His head sinks into his hands.*)

(*Enter GLAGOLYEV through the open door, leaning heavily on a stick, breathing with difficulty.*)

GLAGOLYEV. Platonov? (*PLATONOV lifts his head out of his hands and gazes blankly at GLAGOLYEV.*) Forgive me . . . (*to VOYNITZEV*) Sergey Pavlovich . . . (*to PLATONOV*) Look, this is very awkward . . . (*He glances at VOYNITZEV.*) Very awkward indeed. But I must know! And I must know today! My whole future depends upon your answer . . . Sit down, if I may . . . Walked here . . . Not as well as I might be . . . (*He sits down on the sofa.*) Yes, well . . . You know, of course, that I have long cherished certain hopes with regard to Anna Petrovna . . . In the last few days, however, I have been told certain things . . . It may be mere ru-

mour . . . But they say that Anna Petrovna . . . Or
rather they say that you . . . Or let me put it like this: I
have, as you know, a great respect for women,
but . . . Have pity on me, Platonov . . . !

PLATONOV. I know only one thing, my friend.

GLAGOLYEV. Yes?

PLATONOV. I know that there is nothing but corrup-
tion under the sun. (*PLATONOV picks up the revolver
and goes out.*)

GLAGOLYEV. (*to VOYNITZEV.*) Is this true?

VOYNITZEV. (*lifts his head and registers GLAGO-
LYEV's presence for the first time*) What?

GLAGOLYEV. I realise how painful this is for you. But I
must know! Has she — have they — do you know of any
circumstance that might unfit her to be a wife? (*VOYN-
ITZEV weeps.*) I see. I see. Thank you for your frank-
ness. So much for love, then. So much for respect.

(*Enter ANNA PETROVNA through the open door.*)

ANNA PETROVNA. Misha! I can't find him . . . Oh,
you're *here*! What are you doing here?

GLAGOLYEV. I have been taking a lesson from the
schoolmaster. And now I am going forth into the world
to put that lesson into practice. I'm going to start living
before I die! One thing I shall never do, though. I shall
never foul my own nest! I'll do my living in someone
else's backyard!

ANNA PETROVNA. I thought you were going to catch
the evening train?

GLAGOLYEV. I *am* going to catch the evening train! To
Paris! (*Exit GLAGOLYEV, slamming the door behind
him.*)

ANNA PETROVNA. To Paris . . . ? Sergey, we've lost

the estate! What's happened? What are you doing here? What have you been telling him?

VOYNITZEV. Nothing. He was talking to Platonov.

ANNA PETROVNA. Platonov? And Platonov told him . . . ? What did Platonov tell him?

VOYNITZEV. I wasn't listening.

ANNA PETROVNA. You weren't listening? You just sat there and did nothing while they took the estate away from you? God gave this estate to your ancestors! Now people walk in and take it away from you again — and you don't even ask them why!

VOYNITZEV. I don't care about the estate.

ANNA PETROVNA. Sergey! Where are we going to go? What are we going to eat? We're finished!

VOYNITZEV. I've lost something infinitely more precious to me than the estate. I've love my wife.

ANNA PETROVNA. What do you mean, you've lost your wife? She was alive and well half-an-hour ago — I saw her!

VOYNITZEV. She's in love with someone else.

ANNA PETROVNA. Don't be silly. Concentrate on the estate . . . How *could* she be in love with someone else? There's no one in this miserable little place to be in love with! There's only the doctor. She's not in love with the doctor! There are only a few elderly landowners and a retired colonel and . . . Oh, no!

VOYNITZEV. Yes.

ANNA PETROVNA. No, no! That's not possible! I can tell you that for a fact!

VOYNITZEV. She's his mistress. She told me herself.

ANNA PETROVNA. Oh no. Oh no . . . (*She sits down.*) But what could he possibly see in her? And what were *you* doing, pray? You're supposed to be her husband! Have you no eyes in your head? You just sit there snivelling while they take the world away all round you! What sort of man are you? Anyway, Platonov isn't in love with her. He's seduced her, that's all. He doesn't love her, I can assure you of that! In fact, I see now what he's running away from . . . He's leaving tonight. Did you know that?

VOYNITZEV. They're leaving together.

ANNA PETROVNA. Nonsense! Sofya's at home! I saw her!

(The door is flung open. SOFYA stands on the threshold, with a suitcase, hatboxes, ulsters, etc..)

SOFYA. (*bitterly*) Your word of honour, Platonov! You gave me your word of honour! (*She comes face to face with ANNA PETROVNA and VOYNITZEV. Pause.*)

ANNA PETROVNA. What fools men are! A flutter of the eyelashes, and their back's broken! I'm sorry, Sergey.

VOYNITZEV. I'm going to shoot myself.

SOFYA. (*quietly*) Where is he?

VOYNITZEV. Where's my revolver?

ANNA PETROVNA. What could he begin to see in a little ninny like you? I'm sorry, but that's what you are —an insipid little ninny!

SOFYA. Where is he?

ANNA PETROVNA. And now you've lost him again!

VOYNITZEV. I've lost my revolver.

ANNA PETROVNA. Your revolver?

VOYNITZEV. I put it on the table.

ANNA PETROVNA. Your estate — your wife — your revolver . . . ! Can't you keep your hands on anything?

Voynitzev. He must have picked it up, and . . .
Sofya. (*urgently*) Where is he? (*A shot, off.*)
Anna Petrovna. (*to VOYNITZEV*) You've killed him.
Sofya. (*to VOYNITZEV*) You gave him your revolver.
Anna Petrovna. You put it on the table in front of him.
Sofya. You watched him pick it up.
Voynitzev. No!
Anna Petrovna. They you cold-bloodedly sat here.
Voynitzev. No!
Sofya. And waited.
Voynitzev. No! No!
Anna Petrovna. And kept us talking until . . .

(*Enter PLATONOV. He crosses in silence to the table and puts the revolver back on it.*)

Platonov. They've shot him.
Anna Petrovna. Platonov!
Sofya. Are you all right?
Platonov. It was the peasants. They've shot him!

(*TWO PEASANTS approach the window, dragging something that remains out of sight.*)

First Peasant. Sitting on a tree-stump, he was.
Second Peasant. Gazing at the old schoolhouse.
Fist Peasant. Didn't run. Didn't move.
Second Peasant. Reckon he'd gone a bit soft in the head.
First Peasant. Want to see him? (*They haul the*

dead OSIP up above the level of the window-ledge by his hair.)

ANNA PETROVNA. Osip!

SOFYA. Horrible! Horrible!

VOYNITZEV. Take him away! (*The TWO PEASANTS drop OSIP out of sight. They drag the body away. PLATONOV pours himself vodka.*)

ANNA PETROVNA. Poor Osip! He used to bring me baby birds. He tried to kiss me once.

SOFYA. (*to PLATONOV*) That could have been you, lying dead out there. (*PLATONOV drinks.*)

VOYNITZEV. If he were half a man, it would be.

ANNA PETROVNA. Yes, now listen, Platonov . . .

SOFYA. It's after eight! You gave me your word of honour!

PLATONOV. (*holds up his hand*) I haven't come back to listen to reproaches. I've come back because I discovered something important while I was standing out there with the gun in my hand. I looked at Osip lying there in his blood and I knew for certain: I don't want to die! I looked death in the face; and I chose life! I know you're all unhappy. But what about me? I've lost everything! My honour — my home — my loved ones! I know you're all suffering torments. But think of me, standing out there with the gun in my hand, agonising between life and death! I come back to you hoping to be understood — I throw myself on your mercy — and what happens? You attack me like wild animals! All right — I apologise! I beg your forgiveness! What more do you want of me? Wasn't that one accursed night and all its consequences enough for you? My arm hurts — I'm as hungry as a starving dog — I'm cold — I'm ill — I'm shaking with fever — I'm going to lie down. (*He lies down on the sofa.*)

I'm not going out again. It's raining out there. (*Pause. They all gaze at him.*)

SOFYA. Why are we standing here?

ANNA PETROVNA. Yes, are we bewitched?

VOYNITZEV. Platonov, are you running or aren't you?

ANNA PETROVNA. And if so with whom?

(*Enter COLONEL TRILETZKY.*)

COLONEL TRILETZKY. She's taken poison! She's swallowed the matches!

PLATONOV. (*sits up*) Sasha?

SOFYA. Oh, no!

ANNA PETROVNA. She's not . . . ?

COLONEL TRILETZKY. She would be, if her brother hadn't found her. He's trying to save her. Mishenka, I beg you — go to her! Never mind what's happened. Just go to her and tell her you love her! Comfort her, Misha! Help us to save her!

PLATONOV. (*tries to get up and fails*) Can't stand. Can't get my balance.

COLONEL TRILETZKY. Misha! Please!

PLATONOV. I'm ill, too, Father-in-law! I'm a sick man! I'm on fire! Water! Give me some water! (*COLONEL TRILETZKY hands him a jug. PLATONOV drinks straight from it.*)

ANNA PETROVNA. He's drunk. I'll go.

SOFYA. *I'll* go.

ANNA PETROVNA. You?

SOFYA. I'll beg her to forgive me! (*Exit SOFYA.*)

ANNA PETROVNA. Sofya! Come back! (*Exit ANNA PETROVNA after SOFYA.*)

VOYNITZEV. Anna Petrovna! Sofya! Both of you! Don't make things any worse . . . ! (*Exit VOYNITZEV after ANNA PETROVNA.*)

COLONEL TRILETZKY. My only daughter, Misha!

PLATONOV. I'm a swine! I'm such a swine!

COLONEL TRILETZKY. My little girl, Misha!

PLATONOV. But, my God, I've been punished for it! Well and truly punished!

COLONEL TRILETZKY. Don't keep her waiting, Misha! She's sinking!

PLATONOV. I can scarcely hold my head up on my shoulders! Look, it's going to fall off!

COLONEL TRILETZKY. It's nothing. Misha. You've been drinking, that's all.

PLATONOV. No, I've got a fever. I've been out in the rain.

COLONEL TRILETZKY. It's not raining, Misha.

PLATONOV. I can't see any thing. All I can see is little soldiers. Little green and yellow soldiers in pointed caps. They're crawling over everything . . . ! I need a doctor! Get me a doctor! (*Enter GREKOVA through the open door.*)

COLONEL TRILETZKY. Wait there, Misha. I'll tell Kolya. (*to GREKOVA*) Look after him. He's ill. And Sasha's ill. (*to PLATONOV*) I'll see if Kolya can leave Sasha for a moment . . . (*Exit COLONEL TRILETZKY.*)

PLATONOV. (*flaps his hand in front of his eyes*). All these flies everywhere! Clouds of flies! I can't see any-thing! Shoot the flies . . . (*He picks up the revolver.*)

GREKOVA. (*points the revolver at her*) Who's this?

GREKOVA. It's me!

PLATONOV. The doctor, is it?

GREKOVA. Marya Yefimovna!

PLATONOV. Can't see you. Flies everywhere.

GREKOVA. Beetle-juice!

PLATONOV. Beetle-juice? My mortal enemy! (*He points the revolver.*)

GREKOVA. No! No! I got your message!

PLATONOV. Message?

GREKOVA. I meet him at the ford — I had the pony and trap — I've galloped all the way . . . I just want to say, don't! Please don't!

PLATONOV. Don't what?

GREKOVA. You said you were . . . going away. Going away forever. I knew at once. Please don't! (*She holds out her hand for the revolver.*) Please give it to me!

PLATONOV. I'm ill. I've got a fever.

GREKOVA. I'll look after you.

PLATONOV. Got to have water.

GREKOVA. I'll give you water. (*She picks up the jug.*) If you give me that.

PLATONOV. Water . . . Water . . . (*He exchanges the revolver for the jug, and drinks.*)

GREKOVA. Thank God I got here in time!

PLATONOV. I can't stay here. I've got to get to bed.

GREKOVA. I'll put you to bed in my house. I've got the trap outside.

PLATONOV. Quickly! Quickly! Help me! (*GREKOVA puts the revolver down, safely out of his reach, and goes to him.*) Hand! Give my your hand . . . ! Oh, cold hand! Lovely hand! Kiss your lovely cold hand . . .

GREKOVA. No, no . . .

PLATONOV. And your lovely cold cheek . . . (*He pulls her down into his lap and kisses her cheek.*)

GREKOVA. You mustn't do that.

PLATONOV. I'm not going to seduce you, my dear! No fit state at the moment. Can't even see you properly . . . Can't see you, but I love you all the same. (*He kisses her hands.*)

GREKOVA. I know what happened. It was Sofya, wasn't it.

PLATONOV. Sofya, Zizi, Mimi, Masha . . . I love everyone—and everyone loves me. I insult them, I treat them abominably—and they love me just the same! (*He puts his arm round her.*) Take that Beetle-juice girl, for example. I indecently assaulted her—I kissed her . . . (*He kisses her.*) . . . and she's still in love with me . . . Oh, you are Beetle-juice, aren't you. Sorry.

GREKOVA. You're all muddled up inside that head of yours. (*She embraces him. He flinches.*) You're in pain, too. Tell me where it hurts.

PLATONOV. In Platonov—that's where it hurts . . . *Are* you in love with me, then? Are you really?

GREKOVA. Yes. (*She kisses him.*) I am in love with you.

PLATONOV. Yes, they're all in love with me. Once I used to moralise away to them all, and they loved me for it. Now I seduce them instead, and they still love me.

GREKOVA. You do what you like with me. I don't mind. (*She weeps.*) You're only human, after all. And that's enough for me.

(*Enter DR. TRILETZKY.*)

DR. TRILETZKY. (*cheerfully*) Misha! We've got a surprise for you! (*He freezes at the sight of GREKOVA sitting in PLATONOV's lap.*)

(*Enter SASHA, supported by ANNA PETROVNA and SOFYA, and followed by VOYNITZEV and COLONEL TRILETZKY.*)

ANNA PETROVNA. (*to SASHA*) Come on, my dear. You know you want to see him.

SOFYA. (*to SASHA*) You know *he* wants to see you . . . (*The women halt at the spectacle before them.*)

VOYNITZEV. Terrible tragedy!

COLONEL TRILETZKY. But it's got a happy ending. (*VOYNITZEV and COLONEL TRILETZKY halt in their turn. GREKOVA hides her face in PLATONOV's neck. PLATONOV hugs her, unaware of his audience.*)

PLATONOV. No fit state now. Never you fear, though —when I get better again I'll seduce you like the rest of them. (*DR. TRILETZKY is the first to move.*)

DR. TRILETZKY. Misha! If I've told you once I've told you a thousand times . . . !

SOFYA. The revolver! Where's the revolver? (*She finds it and points it at PLATOMOV.*)

GREKOVA. (*jumps up and interposes herself between SOFYA and PLATONOV*) No! No!

VOYNITZEV. Sofya! It was all going to be all right!

ANNA PETROVNA. (*tries to take the revolver from SOFYA*) Give me that! I'll do it myself!

GREKOVA. I love him!

SASHA. (*left unsupported, sinks to her knees*) Kill me! Not him!

COLONEL TRILETZKY. (*vacillates uncertainly between SASHA and the others*) Sasha . . . ! Sofya Yegorovna . . . !

DR. TRILETZKY. Misha!

VOYNITZEV. Sofya!

COLONEL TRILETZKY. Kolya . . . ! Sasha . . . !

GREKOVA. We love each other!

SOFYA. (*in a terrible voice*) Stand back! All of you!

(*Enter MARKO through the open door.*)

PLATONOV. Wait! What does *he* want? (*They all turn and see MARKO.*)

MARKO. Three rubles.

PLATONOV. Three rubles?

MARKO. If you're happy, sir.

PLATONOV. Happy? My cup runneth over! Give him four! (*In the instant while they automatically feel in their pockets and look around for four rubles, PLATONOV jumps out of the window. SOFYA and the others rush to the window after him. As they do so there is the sound of an approaching train whistle, and they all turn, struck by the same thought. They run out of the door, shouting after PLATONOV; and the world falls apart. Amidst the gathering roar of the train the rear wall of the house moves aside and the lights go down. The forest and the railway line of the previous scene are revealed beyond, with everyone going away upstage, searching and calling PLATONOV's name. PLATONOV emerges from the shadows behind their backs. He steps on to the railway line and runs in the opposite direction — downstage — glancing back over his shoulder at them like a fugitive. Then he stops, blinded by the brilliant headlight of the train approaching from behind the heads of the audience, its whistle screaming. He staggers back a step or two, trying to wave the train away like the flies. Then sudden blackness, and the great roar of the train, its note falling as it passes us. The red tail light of the train appears at the front of the stage and dwindles rapidly into the smoke left by the locomotive. There is a smell of sulphur in the air.*)

Curtain.

Other Publications for Your Interest

NOISES OFF
(LITTLE THEATRE—FARCE)

By MICHAEL FRAYN

5 men, 4 women—2 Interiors

This wonderful Broadway smash hit is "a farce about farce, taking the clichés of the genre and shaking them inventively through a series of kaleidoscopic patterns. Never missing a trick, it has as its first act a pastiche of traditional farce; as its second, a contemporary variant on the formula; as its third, an elaborate undermining of it. The play opens with a touring company dress-rehearsing 'Nothing On', a conventional farce. Mixing mockery and homage, Frayn heaps into this play-within-a-play a hilarious melee of stock characters and situations. Caricatures—cheery char, outraged wife and squeaky blonde—stampede in and out of doors. Voices rise and trousers fall . . . a farce that makes you think as well as laugh."—London Times Literary Supplement. ". . . as side-splitting a farce as I have seen. Ever? *Ever.*"—John Simon, NY Magazine. "The term 'hilarious' must have been coined in the expectation that something on the order of this farce-within-a-farce would eventually come along to justify it."—N.Y. Daily News. "Pure fun."—N.Y. Post. "A joyous and loving reminder that the theatre really does go on, even when the show falls apart."—N.Y. Times. (#16052)

(Royalty, $60–$40 when available.)

THE REAL THING
(ADVANCED GROUPS—COMEDY)

By TOM STOPPARD

4 men, 3 women—Various settings

The effervescent Mr. Stoppard has never been more intellectually—and *emotionally*—engaging than in this "backstage" comedy about a famous playwright named Henry Boot whose second wife, played on Broadway to great acclaim by Glenn Close (who won the Tony Award), is trying to merge "worthy causes" (generally a euphemism for left-wing politics) with her art as an actress. She has met a "political prisoner" named Brodie who has been jailed for radical thuggery, and who has written an inept play about how property is theft, about how the State stifles the Rights of The Individual, etc., etc., etc. Henry's wife wants him to make the play work theatrically, which he does after much soul-searching. Eventually, though, he is able to convince his wife that Brodie is emphatically *not* a victim of political repression. He is, in fact, a *thug*. Famed British actor Jeremy Irons triumphed in the Broadway production (Tony Award), which was directed to perfection by none other than Mike Nichols (Tony Award). "So densely and entertainingly packed with wit, ideas and feelings that one visit just won't do . . . Tom Stoppard's most moving play and the most bracing play anyone has written about love and marriage in years."—N.Y. Times. "Shimmering, dazzling theatre, a play of uncommon wit and intelligence which not only thoroughly delights but challenges and illuminates our lives."—WCBS-TV. 1984 Tony Award-Best Play. (#941)

(Royalty, $60–$40 when available.)

Other Publications for Your Interest

HUSBANDRY

(LITTLE THEATRE—DRAMA)

By PATRICK TOVATT

2 men, 2 women—Interior

At its recent world premiere at the famed Actors Theatre of Louisville, this enticing new drama moved an audience of theatre professionals up off their seats and on to their feet to cheer. Mr. Tovatt has given us an insightful drama about what is happening to the small, family farm in America—and what this means for the future of the country. The scene is a farmhouse whose owners are on the verge of losing their farm. They are visited by their son and his wife, who live "only" eight hours' drive away. The son has a good job in the city, and his wife does, too. The son, Harry, is really put on the horns of a dilemma when he realizes that he is his folks' only hope. The old man can't go it alone anymore—and he needs his son. Pulling at him from the other side is his wife, who does not want to leave her job and uproot her family to become a farm wife. *Husbandry*, then, is ultimately about what it means to be a *husband*—both in the farm and in the family sense. *Variety* praised the "delicacy of Tovatt's dialogue", and called the play "a literate exploration of family responsibilities in a mobile society." Said *Time*: "The play simmers so gently for so long, as each potential confrontation is deflected with Chekhovian shrugs and silences, that when it boils into hostility it sears the audience."   (#10169)

(Royalty, $60-$40.)

CLARA'S PLAY

(LITTLE THEATRE—DRAMA)

By JOHN OLIVE

3 men, 1 woman—Exterior

Clara, an aging spinster, lives alone in a remote farmhouse. She is the last surviving member of one of the area's most prominent families. It is summer, 1915. Enter an immigrant, feisty soul named Sverre looking for a few days' work before moving on. But Clara's farm needs more than just a few days' work, and Sverre stays on to help Clara fix up and run the farm. It soon becomes clear unscrupulous local businessmen are bilking Clara out of money and hope to gain control of her property. Sverre agrees to stay on to help Clara keep her family's property. "A story of determination, loyalty. It has more than a measure of love, of resignation, of humor and loyalty."—Chicago Sun-Times. "A playwright of unusual sensitivity in delineating character and exploring human relationships." —Chicago Tribune. "Gracefully-written, with a real sense of place."—Village Voice. A recent success both at Chicago's fine Wisdom Bridge Theatre and at the Great American Play Festival of the world-reknowned Actors Theatre of Louisville; and, on tour, starring Jean Stapleton.   (#5076)

(Royalty, $50-$35.)

Other Publications for Your Interest

A WEEKEND NEAR MADISON
(LITTLE THEATRE—COMIC DRAMA)

By KATHLEEN TOLAN

2 men, 3 women—Interior

This recent hit from the famed Actors Theatre of Louisville, a terrific ensemble play about male-female relationships in the 80's, was praised by *Newsweek* as "warm, vital, glowing . . . full of wise ironies and unsentimental hopes". The story concerns a weekend reunion of old college friends now in their early thirties. The occasion is the visit of Vanessa, the queen bee of the group, who is now the leader of a lesbian/feminist rock band. Vanessa arrives at the home of an old friend who is now a psychiatrist hand in hand with her naif-like lover, who also plays in the band. Also on hand are the psychiatrist's wife, a novelist suffering from writer's block; and his brother, who was once Vanessa's lover and who still loves her. In the course of the weekend, Vanessa reveals that she and her lover desperately want to have a child—and she tries to persuade her former male lover to father it, not understanding that he might have some feelings about the whole thing. *Time Magazine* heard "the unmistakable cry of an infant hit . . . Playwright Tolan's work radiates promise and achievement." (#25051)

(Royalty, $60-$40.)

PASTORALE
(LITTLE THEATRE—COMEDY)

By DEBORAH EISENBERG

3 men, 4 women—Interior
(plus 1 or 2 bit parts and 3 optional extras)

"Deborah Eisenberg is one of the freshest and funniest voices in some seasons."—Newsweek. Somewhere out in the country Melanie has rented a house and in the living room she, her friend Rachel who came for a weekend but forgets to leave, and their school friend Steve (all in their mid-20s) spend nearly a year meandering through a mental landscape including such concerns as phobias, friendship, work, sex, slovenliness and epistemology. Other people happen by: Steve's young girlfriend Celia, the virtuous and annoying Edie, a man who Melanie has picked up in a bar, and a couple who appear during an intense conversation and observe the sofa is on fire. The lives of the three friends inevitably proceed and eventually draw them, the better prepared perhaps by their months on the sofa, in separate directions. "The most original, funniest new comic voice to be heard in New York theater since Beth Henley's 'Crimes of the Heart.'"—N.Y. Times. "A very funny, stylish comedy."—The New Yorker. "Wacky charm and wayward wit."—New York Magazine. "Delightful."—N.Y. Post. "Uproarious . . . the play is a world unto itself, and it spins."—N.Y. Sunday Times. (#18016)

(Royalty, $50-$35.)

Other Publications for Your Interest

TALKING WITH . . .
(LITTLE THEATRE)

By JANE MARTIN

11 women—Bare stage

Here, at last, is the collection of eleven extraordinary monologues for eleven actresses which had them on their feet cheering at the famed Actors Theatre of Louisville—audiences, critics and, yes, even jaded theatre professionals. The mysteriously pseudonymous Jane Martin is truly a "find", a new writer with a wonderfully idiosyncratic style, whose characters alternately amuse, move and frighten us always, however, speaking to us from the depths of their souls. The characters include a baton twirler who has found God through twirling; a fundamentalist snake handler, an ex-rodeo rider crowded out of the life she has cherished by men in 3-piece suits who want her to dress up "like Minnie damn Mouse in a tutu"; an actress willing to go to any length to get a job; and an old woman who claims she once saw a man with "cerebral walrus" walk into a McDonald's and be healed by a Big Mac. "Eleven female monologues, of which half a dozen verge on brilliance."—London Guardian. "Whoever (Jane Martin) is, she's a writer with an original imagination."—Village Voice. "With Jane Martin, the monologue has taken on a new poetic form, intensive in its method and revelatory in its impact."—Philadelphia Inquirer. "A dramatist with an original voice . . . (these are) tales about enthusiasms that become obsessions, eccentric confessionals that levitate with religious symbolism and gladsome humor."—N.Y. Times. *Talking With* . . . is the 1982 winner of the American Theatre Critics Association Award for Best Regional Play. (#22009)

(Royalty, $60-$40.
If individual monologues are done separately: Royalty, $15-$10.)

HAROLD AND MAUDE
(ADVANCED GROUPS—COMEDY)

By COLIN HIGGINS

9 men, 8 women—Various settings

Yes: the *Harold and Maude!* This is a stage adaptation of the wonderful movie about the suicidal 19 year-old boy who finally learns how to truly *live* when he meets up with that delightfully whacky octogenarian, Maude. Harold is the proverbial Poor Little Rich Kid. His alienation has caused him to attempt suicide several times, though these attempts are more cries for attention than actual attempts. His peculiar attachment to Maude, whom he meets at a funeral (a mutual passion), is what saves him—and what captivates us. This new stage version, a hit in France directed by the internationally-renowned Jean-Louis Barrault, will certainly delight both afficionados of the film and new-comers to the story. "Offbeat upbeat comedy."—Christian Science Monitor. (#10032)

(Royalty, $60-$40.)

Other Publications for Your Interest

THE CURATE SHAKESPEARE AS YOU LIKE IT
(LITTLE THEATRE—COMEDY)
By DON NIGRO

4 men, 3 women—Bare stage

This extremely unusual and original piece is subtitled: "The record of one company's attempt to perform the play by William Shakespeare". When the very prolific Mr. Nigro was asked by a professional theatre company to adapt *As You Like It* so that it could be performed by a company of seven he, of course, came up with a completely original play about a rag-tag group of players comprised of only seven actors led by a dotty old curate who nonetheless must present Shakespeare's play; and the dramatic interest, as well as the comedy, is in their hilarious attempts to impersonate all of Shakespeare's multitude of characters. The play has had numerous productions nationwide, all of which have come about through word of mouth. We are very pleased to make this "underground comic classic" widely available to theatre groups who like their comedy wide open and theatrical. (#5742)

(Royalty, $50–$25.)

SEASCAPE WITH SHARKS AND DANCER
(LITTLE THEATRE—DRAMA)
By DON NIGRO

1 man, 1 woman—Interior

This is a fine new play by an author of great talent and promise. We are very glad to be introducing Mr. Nigro's work to a wide audience with *Seascape With Sharks and Dancer*, which comes directly from a sold-out, critically acclaimed production at the world-famous Oregon Shakespeare Festival. The play is set in a beach bungalow. The young man who lives there has pulled a lost young woman from the ocean. Soon, she finds herself trapped in his life and torn between her need to come to rest somewhere and her certainty that all human relationships turn eventually into nightmares. The struggle between his tolerant and gently ironic approach to life and her strategy of suspicion and attack becomes a kind of war about love and creation which neither can afford to lose. In other words, this is quite an offbeat, wonderful love story. We would like to point out that the play also contains a wealth of excellent *monologue* and *scene material.* (#21060)

(Royalty, $50–$35.)